GOOD LISTENING

Good Listening

by

R. D. DARRELL

NEW YORK: ALFRED A. KNOPF

1 9 5 3

L. C. catalog card number: 52-12187

THIS IS A BORZOI BOOK, PUBLISHED BY

ALFRED A. KNOPF, INC.

FIRST EDITION

To the many friends

over many years with whom I have
listened to and argued about music
on records.

And in particular to two of the best
(friends, listeners, and arguers):

Charlotte & Richard Gilbert

Contents

CONTENTS

PART III
One World—Many Mansions

GOOD LISTENING

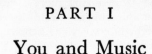

PART I

You and Music

1. Lead-In Grooves

> *A man may see how this world goes*
> *with no eyes. Look with thine ears.*
> —SHAKESPEARE: *King Lear*

MUSIC, for most people, seems to be a thing of strange delight shrouded in stranger mystery. Perhaps no other art is worshipped so timidly, even by those most magnetically attracted to it. Certainly no other gives rise to such a sharp contradiction as that between an avid "love" for music and an apologetic confession of musical incapacity, so characteristic of today's mass audiences.

Great as their enjoyment may be, most listeners nourish a peculiar inferiority complex. If their self-diagnosis is to be believed, their "appreciation" is almost hopelessly handicapped by some innate deficiency in musical aptitude, or at least by a lack of formal training. But whether these weaknesses are real or imaginary, the patients' descriptions of their own ills provide a remarkably inaccurate index to the actual state of their musical health. For the facts are that more non-professionals listen more regularly nowadays, and listen to more and better music, than ever before in history.

Much of the mystery can be cleared up, I am firmly convinced, simply by recognizing that a music-*maker's* special skills are by no means essential (however helpful they may

be) to a non-professional *listener;* by understanding better
the roles played by heredity and environment in everyone's
musical life; and by realizing more clearly the changes
that have almost miraculously transformed both today's
musical world and contemporary listeners' opportunities.

Now, it is extremely unlikely that the natural heritage
of a modern baby differs markedly from that of one born
in, say, medieval times. Individuals always have varied
widely where musical inclinations and aptitudes are concerned. But no one—not even a young Bach or Mozart—
is so gifted at birth that there is nothing left for him to
learn. And no one—not even the totally deaf—is born in-
capable of musical learning. The absence of specialized
psychological or physical attributes certainly seems to rule
out a professional musician's career, though even such disadvantages can be and have been overcome. But in the
enjoyment—rather than the actual making—of music, no
one ever is insuperably handicapped.

No matter what your sense of musical "inferiority," no
matter whether or not you can sing or play, you, like everyone else, always can *listen*—even if it is only by "feeling"
sound vibrations. And all of us who really want to can
always find something to listen to—often something that
provides not merely momentary enjoyment, but incomparable invigoration and enrichment of our whole lives.

The fundamental difference between the musical world
of today and that of the past lies in the revolutionary
changes that have taken place *outside* ourselves. Among
these are the enormous expansions in both the quantity
and the quality of readily available music, the enhanced
ease with which listeners are brought into contact with
music-makers, and, perhaps most important of all, the radical shifts in listening locales and conditions—from set programs in public concert halls and opera houses to the music
of our own choice, heard at our own convenience, in our
own homes.

Where once only musicians, trained amateurs, and a select few of high birth or wealth had the privilege of listen-

ing to music regularly, now almost anyone can listen when and as often as he likes. And where until comparatively recently you were obliged either to make music for yourself or to attend concerts (and the latter normally were necessary if you wanted to hear the best music in performances of professional stature), music of all kinds, much of it in the finest performances of our times, now is readily accessible in recordings and broadcasts.

Of course, not everything is rosy in our brave new world of music. Considerable expense still is involved. There is no direct charge for broadcast listening, to be sure, and long-playing records are remarkably inexpensive in terms of extent and quality of music per dollar. But any extensive record library represents a very substantial investment, and even adequate reproducing equipment is hardly cheap, while really good equipment makes heavy demands in both money and space.

Probably the greatest environmental handicap, however, is our age's insatiable drain on human energy. Business and housekeeping may require far less time and effort than they used to, but in our new-found leisure listening must compete desperately with travel, sports, theatergoing, and— right in our own homes—with the rival attractions of reading and conversation, television, news and dramatic broadcasts.

Nevertheless, all these handicaps and counterappeals obviously are relatively minor problems, at least to anyone genuinely eager to listen to music. They never should blind our realization of the phenomenal advantages we now can boast in ease of access to more and better music, advantages almost incredibly superior to those enjoyed by even the most favored of our ancestors.

Many of us need only look back at our own youth to highlight the profound changes that have occurred. When I first began going to symphony concerts, it took two or three years of regular attendance to hear all the Beethoven symphonies, whereas today I should have no difficulty in hearing all nine, some probably in more than one performance, in less than a week of F-M radio listening. And I was a faithful concertgoer for some years before I heard more than a single Bach choral work—whereas today I can choose in the long-playing-record catalogues among some forty complete cantatas, two Passions, two oratorios, the B minor Mass and D major *Magnificat*, and several short Masses and motets, many of them in more than one recorded edition.

But this point surely needs no argument. The contemporary scope of the recorded repertory and its public is impressively enough displayed in catalogues and discographies, in the advertisements and reviews in magazines and newspapers, in manufacturers' sales-figures and the estimated audiences both for the big networks' concert broadcasts and for independent (particularly F-M) broadcasters' recorded-music programs.

"Canned" music, once derided and despised, as indeed canned foods had been only a generation or two earlier, now is accepted almost as matter-of-factly.

But by a familiar paradox, the abundance of music brings with it new problems, particularly those of possible oversupply and of consumer education. Music literally is "in the air" today. Dulled sensibilities and overstimulated appetites have become disturbing factors, as has that of actual aural fatigue. And of even more direct concern to most listeners (who seldom are conscious of the risk of sheer tonal surfeit) are the bewildering, practical problems of *selection* and *orientation*.

Obviously, we can't buy everything unless we have unlimited pocketbooks, and we couldn't hear it all even if we had unlimited leisure. Without previous musical training, how are we to know what is the "best" music—or how to "appreciate" it even if it is authoritatively preselected? Lacking both background and perspective, how are we to locate ourselves in the whole world of music or chart the paths by which we can venture most easily from familiar into entirely strange territories?

If you happen to be one of the rapidly multiplying

amateur experts in such matters, a musical connoisseur
or "phonophile," say, you'll have your own pat answers to
these questions. Any I advance will afford you only the
satisfaction of confirmation or disputation. I'm writing
here, however, primarily for those who lack either knowledge or confidence, and especially for the admittedly
non-expert—the novice general listeners.

Music, for such listeners, isn't the most important thing
in the world, but it has come to play an increasingly significant part in their lives. While they may feel the familiar
term "music-lover" faintly distasteful or inexact, they are
seriously interested in music—at least to the extent of
wanting to hear more and to get more out of what they
hear. They have begun (probably quite recently) to buy
and enjoy music on records, or to listen regularly to broadcasts of mostly recorded music. Or their record and broadcast listening has been developing more or less haphazardly
to the point where they now realize that a more systematic
approach and wider background knowledge are demanded
for any further intensification and expansion of their
enjoyment.

Yet whatever these listeners may lack in specialized
knowledge, they feel themselves to possess at least normal
intelligence. They don't hanker to be impressed (or confused) by any display of erudition, or to be talked down to
like rather backward schoolboys. What they want most is
specific, practical help—direct help in making the dollars
they spend on records bring better returns, long-term help
in making the time they spend in listening to or in reading
about music contribute more richly to their experience.

This little book is planned to meet as fully and as clearly
as possible some of the most pressing needs of such listener
readers. It assumes that their main listening medium will
be records, heard either on a home phonograph or on a
broadcast receiver. But because attention is focused on
content rather than medium, musical works are discussed
in the text usually without reference to specific recordings.
In the back of the book, however, a combined Index-

Discography supplies a recommended (long-playing) disc edition of each work mentioned—thus serving not only as a conventional index of text references, but also as a carefully selected record-library catalogue.

Shaping the text material to the patterns of growth most characteristic of the current listening public, I begin with the novice's normal, seemingly haphazard, personal approaches to music. And I endeavor to show how his instinctive tastes are by no means entirely arbitrary, but are rooted in (and even predictable from) his individual temperament and earlier experience.

In Part II it is assumed that on reaching some degree of familiarity with the best-known composers the maturing listener will be eager to plan his record library on a more systematic basis, and to extend his acquaintanceship to composers of various historical eras.

Finally, in Part III, I attempt to reconcile these personal and historical approaches, first in locating the specialized repertory where one is most likely to feel musically at home; then in expanding the scope of one's experience along the natural grain of one's own temperament and in learning to listen *participatively*.

It should hardly be necessary to add that no reader can be expected to listen to—much less to buy—all the works discussed in these pages. Because it is impossible to know any reader's exact tastes and experience, I have to suggest as many enjoyment possibilities as I can, in the hope that everyone who explores them, however gingerly, will be sure of making at least an optimum number of rewarding discoveries.

But some readers may welcome fair warning of certain unorthodox, perhaps negative features of this book. It is *not* a textbook in music "appreciation," history, or theory. The concern here is with the direct impact of music on your ears and mind, in leading you *to* works you are likely to enjoy—not in trying to tell you how they were composed or what they mean. My general subject is what usually is called (for lack of better terms) great, classical, or "art" music, but while popular, jazz, and folk works mostly are excluded, that is for brevity only and not on the basis of any arbitrary standards of what is or isn't "good" music.

I believe (fanatically, perhaps) that our record libraries are best chosen to fit our own personal, often highly idiosyncratic musical needs. The last thing I want to do is to make hairsplitting distinctions among what is good, better, and best by my—or any other—standards. Instead, I hope to present a broad range of implicit values—leaving it to you to compare and contrast them in your own minds. If your sensibilities are alert and educable, you aren't likely to stray too far or long from generally accepted evaluations, and when you do, your range of enjoyment well may be all the wider for your personal departures from orthodox discrimination.

The most important thing in listening, I'm convinced, is not the formation of respectful attitudes toward the accepted masterpieces, or the hearing of any kind of music with only lukewarm enthusiasm. It is the vital response to the decisive moments of *revelation*—moments that shock our personalities into full self-awareness and often incandescently illuminate our lives outside as well as in music.

The individual significance of such experiences sometimes may seem out of all proportion to their actual stimuli, which may be music of comparatively negligible artistic worth or the most hackneyed of concert warhorses. More often, perhaps, it is music of supreme stature that acts as the trigger to release forces that have been building up within you, awaiting only the right moment and touch to explode. But in either case the prime value lies in the intensity of the reaction itself. For when you experience such revelations, you will know for yourself what appreciation truly means, and you will realize at last just how good "good listening" can be at its very best.

2. Bandwagon Perambulators

All things in their beginning are good for something.
—GEORGE HERBERT: *Outlandish Proverbs*

JUST where your musical life begins is a matter of chance.
How you start out in the world of tone may color your
later experience, but is unlikely to shape your whole destiny. All you need reckon with at first is the simple fact
of your existence—as a listener—in a particular time and
place.

Time and place are the significant influences. They
largely determine both the general kind of music we have
been exposed to before we begin to listen with true awareness, and the specific kind of music that first jolts us (like
a midwife's slap) into personal musical consciousness.

Not so many years ago the initial stimulus probably
would have been one of the great tunes. Any of these
almost universally favorite airs might have worked the
trick, for they're all much alike (whether they stem from
the classics, folk music, or Broadway hit shows) in direct
melodic appeal and ease of immediate assimilation. Once
heard, they are completely known and well-nigh unforgettable.

In those days most record collections began with, or
soon came to include, operatic highlights (usually starring
Caruso) like "*Celeste Aïda*" from *Aïda*, "*La donna è mobile*"
from *Rigoletto*, "*Vesti la giubba*" from *Pagliacci*, and the Sextet from *Lucia di Lammermoor*. Or perhaps a piano record
of pieces like Paderewski's Minuet in G, Rachmaninoff's
C-sharp minor Prelude, and Liszt's *Liebestraum* No. 3.
Or string-instrumental versions of the "Meditation" from
Thaïs, Saint-Saëns's *La Cygne*, Schumann's *Träumerei*, Tchaikovsky's *Andante Cantabile*, or Bach's "Air for the G string."
Either vocal or instrumental versions of Schubert's *Ave*

Maria and *Serenade*, Brahms's *Wiegenlied*, Handel's "Largo," Tchaikovsky's "None but the lonely heart", the Prize Song from Wagner's *Die Meistersinger*, or the *Londonderry Air*.

Such great tunes as these have lost little of their appeal over the years, though of course new interpreters have risen to stardom. In recent years records have shared some of the vast broadcast and film audiences entranced by Nelson Eddy, Lily Pons, André Kostelanetz's orchestra, and Mario Lanza, the last frankly wearing the somewhat oversize shoes of the "Great Caruso," but all of them mainly dependent on the great-tune repertory.

Yet the repertory itself has not remained entirely static. Iturbi's best-selling disc of the Chopin Polonaise No. 6 won a place even in the juke boxes. Levant has brought bits of Debussy and Khachaturian to listeners who probably never had heard these composers' names before. Many of the leading themes from the standard piano and symphonic repertories have found new hearers under new names in simplified arrangements as popular ballads and dance pieces. And with this steady influx of new material have come a few even more subtly or exotically contoured airs —from the old Shakespearean favorite "Greensleeves" to the delicately impressionistic *Clair de lune* by Debussy.

But while the appeal of tunefulness will always be a primary factor in the popular acceptance of any kind of music, many contemporary listeners have developed appetites for livelier rhythmic animation, stronger colors, and bigger scale than normally are characteristic of the famous great tunes. Whether we are more sophisticated or more naïve than earlier generations (today's more heterogeneous audiences probably are both), we certainly are far more insistent that music be—above anything else—*exciting*. To some extent this demand is reflected in current interpretative styles and the trend to ever lusher and more intricate "arrangements." But it also is reflected in the demand for music that in itself is at once more intensely dramatic and more grandly ambitious in scope.

Of course, the advent of long-playing records has been largely instrumental in the truly revolutionary expansion of the mass audience's capacity to accept full-length works as well as brief airs and snippet excerpts. Yet their triumph never could have been so rapid and complete if a genuine hunger had not already been developed—not merely for longer playing time itself, but also for the uninterrupted performance of bigger musical works.

Combining these new demands for more dramatic and larger-scaled works, we have a good explanation why so many of the younger generation have been most effectively converted to recorded music through a type of composition that excitingly blends the attractions of melodiousness, rhythmic animation, brightly contrasted tone-colors, and theatrical display—the *concerto*.

Popular as piano concertos have been for many years, both in concert halls and on records, it is only quite recently that they have become sure-fire box-office drawing cards and disc best-sellers. The sensational success of the Horowitz-Toscanini Tchaikovsky First Concerto perhaps is outstanding. But that success has typified as well as spurred the newly enhanced popularity of such notable "classical hits" as Rachmaninoff's Second Concerto and Rhapsody on a Theme by Paganini, the Grieg and Schumann concertos, Beethoven's Fifth ("Emperor") and Fourth concertos, Liszt's First, Brahms's Second, the Franck *Variations symphoniques*, and Gershwin's *Rhapsody in Blue*.

Many of the old violin-concerto concert favorites, too, have found a second, lustier youth in the hearts of ever-expanding phonographic audiences. Mendelssohn's and Tchaikovsky's ingratiating concertos lead the way, perhaps, but not far behind are the more serious D major works by Beethoven and Brahms, as well as Lalo's sparkling *Symphonie espagnole*, the lyrical Chausson *Poème*, and sugary Bruch G minor Concerto.

But of course the best-selling showpieces haven't been confined exclusively to concertos. Stokowski's transcriptions probably have done more to make Bach widely known, through records, broadcasts, and the Disney film *Fantasia*, than all the earnest efforts of other Bach proponents in the last century. The admiring audiences for such "standard" symphonic masterpeices as Beethoven's Third, Fifth, Seventh, and Ninth symphonies, Brahms's First and Fourth and Variations on a Theme by Haydn, and Tchaikovsky's Sixth ("*Pathétique*") Symphony have been enormously expanded, in both size and enthusiasm, by the magic of Toscanini's interpretative fame and vitality. And before his death in 1951, Koussevitzky worked similar miracles in winning countless new admirers for Mendelssohn's Fourth ("Italian") Symphony, the Mussorgsky-Ravel *Pictures at an Exhibition*, Prokofiev's "Classical" Symphony, Richard Strauss's *Till Eulenspiegel*, and Tchaikovsky's Fourth and Fifth symphonies and *Romeo and Juliet* Overture.

Most recently, the pre-eminence of "hit" concertos, symphonies, and tone-poems as characteristic expressions of the spirited tempo and taste of our times is being hotly challenged by ballet music. The widespread growth of public interest in staged, filmed, and televised ballet has helped, obviously, but even without that revival the contemporary craving for dramatic impact and kaleidoscopic interplay of colors still might have created such a succession of best-selling recordings as Ansermet's Stravinsky *Petrouchka* and Falla *Three-Cornered Hat*, Stokowski's Tchaikovsky *Sleeping Beauty* and Borodin *Prince Igor* dances, Monteux's Stravinsky *Sacre*, Fiedler's Offenbach-Rosenthal *Gaîté parisienne*, and many others less closely associated with any one conductor.

Recordings like these, while perhaps the biggest and most impressive vehicles, naturally aren't the only bandwagons that have drawn multitudes of new listeners into the phonogrophic parade. Some surely must have got started in the old way, via one or several of the "great tunes." Many beginners must have helped to swell the incredible circulation of Fiedler's (Boston "Pops") and Kostelanetz's recorded series of music of almost every type. The seed of other disc collections often has been one of the immensely popular Broadway hit shows in the recorded versions (generally by the original casts) that have been of such yeoman aid in the mass public's acceptance of long-playing records. Not infrequently, so-called "serious" or "classical" record libraries have been the outgrowth of a collection that began with dance hits, popular ballads, or hot jazz, or perhaps with non-musical recordings of plays, poetry, and sound newsreels like "I Can Hear It Now."

Plainly, nothing is too unlikely to serve as a beginning —neither what generally is considered by orthodox aesthetic standards to be "trivial" nor what by the same standards is thought to be forbiddingly advanced or erudite. Not long ago I visited a prep-school class in music appreciation where Schumann's Piano Concerto succeeded only in setting all the boys squirming restlessly in their chairs. But immediately after class several of these same boys rushed back to their dormitories to listen raptly to their latest extracurricular co-operative record purchase: Berg's *Wozzeck*!

Long before that, however, I had had my first lesson in the contrariness (at least by arbitrary standards) of young listeners' tastes. Pressed into service for what wasn't yet known as "baby-sitting," I could find nothing in the way of "children's" music that even dented the attention of an unruly group of youngsters. But when I gave up in disgust and began playing what I wanted to hear myself, the kids were spellbound by three of what I would have assumed the most unlikely pieces: Delius's *Brigg Fair*, Duke Ellington's *Sophisticated Lady*, and Bach's *Jesu, Joy of Man's Desiring*.

As I've never been able to account convincingly for all of my own tastes, I've long dodged attempting to explain those of others—individually or *en masse*. I firmly believe we all can learn a great deal by examining and trying to analyze our own and others' preferences, but it's seldom easy—or wise—to draw hard and fast conclusions from what may be only circumstantial evidence.

So while the bandwagon approach to music on records may seem the most popular, it isn't necessarily the only one, and still less the best one for everybody. If you happen to be one of those listeners who first awake to music through something far removed (in either direction) from the best-selling "standard masterpieces," you aren't remarkably exceptional and certainly aren't unique.

But you may be lucky. Discovering so early in the game that you don't particularly like (at least just then) what the majority of listeners admire often fosters an independence of choice that is all too rare among musical novices. If you find your first musical love outside the ranks of the mass public's idols, there probably is less chance of its bloom wearing off too soon through incessant repetition of the work in broadcasts, in concerts, and on your friends' phonographs.

And when your sole medium of contact with the exciting new discovery you have made is a record of your own, you gain a memorable lesson in the phonograph's potentialities as a gateway to hitherto unsuspected enjoyment. Perhaps even more significantly, you learn early what often takes most record-buyers years to realize: that for *you*, best-sellers aren't always the best buys, and that your most rewarding, most nearly inexhaustible investments are in music that has a very special, highly *personal* meaning.

3. First Steps and Steppingstones

> *Every step is an end, and every step is a fresh beginning.*
> —GOETHE: *The Elective Affinities*

WHETHER you are trundled into the world of music on a bandwagon perambulator or stumble into it by sheer accident, what matters most is your vivid awareness of the arrival itself. The first conscious glimpse of new horizons may come with only the gentle shock of recognition, the realization of something sensed before, but never with such sharpened insight. Or it may come with the stronger shock of *revelation*, the blinding illumination of Saul's vision on the road to Damascus. But whether you are part of a vast crowd or a solitary adventurer, the music suddenly revealed to you should have the special validity and force of a wholly individual discovery.

For this is the supreme worth of the phonograph as a medium of musical experience. Its utility lies in making music more accessible; its unique power lies in restoring seemingly direct communication between composer and listener. Actually, of course, the composer may have died centuries ago, the line of communication may be exceedingly long and tortuous, and at the very moment you are listening, thousands of others may have duplicate recordings spinning on their own turntables. Yet such facts have no reality within the closed circle of your own absorption. All you are aware of is that right here—in your own room and in your own ears and mind—music is coming to vibrant life, speaking directly, solely, and intimately to *you*.

This first rapture, like all great thrills, seldom can be recaptured. Although you will come to know your particular musical revelation far better, with your pleasure enriched by repeated hearings, it never again can be so incandescent as in its first discovery. Whatever other experiences may lie in store for you, if you haven't known this one, your musical life never can be quite complete.

The impetus of an auspicious entry into the world of music usually will carry even the novice listener well on his way to mature citizenship. But many potential citizens, strongly attracted by a promised land of musical enjoyment, fail to find a vehicle (bandwagon or other) to carry them through its gates. And there are others who, after having entered successfully, soon find themselves at a loss, bewildered and confused by the strange customs and language of their adopted land.

In either case, it's a natural first instinct to look desperately around for help—help from friends, musical educators, and books. The fact that you are reading these pages itself implies that you are seeking some sort of guidance and have at least hope of finding it here.

I must confess, perhaps rather disconcertingly, that telling anyone what records he should hear and own always has struck me as a rank presumption—even though I've spent most of my life doing just that! Nevertheless, the fact that I and quite a few colleagues have been able to make a living as phonographic "mentors" surely proves that mentors are needed. Indeed, I've been constantly reminded over many years that novice listeners have an insatiable appetite for useful suggestions and advice— from which of course they pick and choose whatever best fits their particular needs. And I've found that perhaps the most rewarding function of a phono-musical guide, certainly his first obligation, is to satisfy the often inarticulate but nonetheless avid hunger for good "introductory" works, suggested steppingstones leading the easiest possible way into the enticing but labyrinthine realm of great music.

The safest choices, for both guide and novice, obviously are the popular bandwagons—those mentioned in the previous chapter, plus other time-tested favorites, such as the following short, readily grasped, "easy classics":

Beethoven's *Egmont* and *Coriolanus* overtures, Bizet's *Carmen* suite, Brahms's *Academic Festival Overture*, Grieg's *Peer Gynt* suites, Humperdinck's *Hänsel und Gretel* prelude, Liszt's *Les Préludes*, Mozart's *Eine kleine Nachtmusik*, Prokofiev's *Peter and the Wolf*, Schubert's *Rosamunde* overture, Smetana's *The Moldau*, Richard Strauss's *Der Rosenkavalier* waltzes, Tchaikovsky's *Nutcracker Suite*, Wagner's *Lohengrin* and *Die Meistersinger* preludes, *Tannhäuser* overture, and *Tristan* Prelude and Love-death.

And for slightly larger-scaled, but hardly more "difficult" works: Bach's Suite No. 3 and Double Violin Concerto, Beethoven's First and Eighth symphonies, Dvořák's Fifth ("New World") Symphony, Franck's D minor Symphony, Haydn's 94th ("Surprise") Symphony, Ravel's *Ma Mère l'Oye*, Schubert's Eighth ("Unfinished") Symphony and Trio Op. 99, Sibelius's First Symphony, Richard Strauss's *Don Juan*, and Tchaikovsky's Fourth Symphony.

Yet, successful as such standard masterpieces always have been and probably always will be, I feel that acting only as one more of their many barker promoters evades a guide's higher duties. While almost everyone succumbs to the lure of bandwagons on occasion and many people never can travel happily on less crowded, more erratically scheduled vehicles, there never has been any lack of bandwagon advertising promotion. But those constitutionally adverse to joining what seems to them like a mob have far more difficulty in finding steppingstone approaches fitted to their own individual tastes and needs.

Lacking any information on such listeners' personal taste-bents, of course I can't know exactly what's best for any specific individual to begin with. When this problem initially faced me, I could only suggest those works which, if all my own records were lost, I'd want to replace first. But with these as a nucleus and on the basis of observed results, I've gradually accumulated a fair-sized batch of recommendations which, though by no means mass-public bandwagons, do appeal strongly to a wide variety of highly individualized tastes. Naturally, I can't predict flatly that you, or anyone, is sure to find lively pleasure in all the following steppingstones. But judging by many listeners' experience, the odds are high that you'll relish most of them. They're works of such marked and reliable attractiveness that when the very first hearing doesn't uncover their full charms, comparatively few repetitions ever are necessary—even for the rankest novice—to reveal them.

For the reasons advanced earlier, this list also begins with concertos—but not the big showpieces best suited for bandwagons. These are far less pretentious, far more "personal" in their appeal. Their color-schemes are simpler, purer, more delicate. And if their drama is less heroic, it often gains in poignance by a more intimate projection on a smaller stage.

Let's start, then, with a little disc of pure magic: the Mozart Horn concertos, K.417 and K.495, with Dennis Brain as soloist in inexpressibly heart-tugging tone-adventures of a golden-voiced protagonist setting forth to explore the world of melody from its sunniest, most fragrant fields to the darker recesses of its enchanted woods.

You may not know a French horn from a Klaxon or may never consciously have heard a work by Mozart, but after listening to these irresistible little works, you'll never be able to forget the instrument's characteristic nobility, sonority, and tonal warmth, and you're likely to realize that in Mozart you've made not only the acquaintance but the fast friendship of one of the most entrancing personalities in all music.

If you find there's something in your imagination that makes a special response to the interplay of tone-coloring here, you can hardly do better than to proceed at once to several other wind-instrument concertos: the more sharply focused, gleaming tones of the trumpet, in Haydn's Concerto and Bach's Brandenburg Concerto No. 2, for example; the huskier voice of the hardly all-comic "clown of the orchestra" in Mozart's bassoon concertos; the pure, silvery tones of the flute in one of Mozart's concertos or Bach's Brandenburg No. 4; or the still differently distinctive tones of the clarinet and oboe, again in concertos by Mozart, or in his Clarinet Quintet and Oboe Quartet.

If it's primarily the protean personality of the composer himself (rather than the tonal "personalities" of his instruments) that strikes your fancy, you should be curious to hear what he can do on a larger scale in his piano concertos. One of the finest single discs I know is the coupling of his K.491 and K.595 concertos by Paul Badura-Skoda with a Viennese orchestra under Prohaska. Here again, underneath this music's apparent simplicity and "innocent" songfulness, are depths of feeling that perhaps can never be fully explored.

Don't worry too much, here or elsewhere in your first musical explorations, about identifying all the thematic or instrumental "characters" in the complex interplay of tonal plots and counterplots. And worry even less about the sound-dramas' "stories" or "meanings." These concertos may be considered miniature operas, for which there are no librettos and no singers, except the instruments themselves. What they are all "about" is simply music-making —the sheerly tonal expression of the eternal human feelings of gaiety, humor, sadness, and courage. No one can tell their meaning—except Mozart himself in his music itself! And the essential first step in "understanding" any music is *responsive attention*—a full sense of the building up and resolution of emotional tensions, by which we deeply feel as well as hear everything the composer is saying.

On the other hand, don't be discouraged if, on first tasting, the Mozartean spring-waters seem disconcertingly cool. In time you'll probably come back to them and change your mind, but meanwhile your tastes apparently demand richer melodic sentiment and coloring, qualities few composers have combined better, or invested with more lyrical magic, than Johann Strauss.

Not, I hasten to stress, the "Waltz King" of best-selling American records—most of which, when the original scoring is not brutally mutilated, are performed with callous insensitivity to their very life-pulse of toe- and heart-tickling true Viennese rhythm. Here is one instance where the band-wagon approach should be avoided like poison. If you know Strauss's waltzes only in the recordings by Kostelanetz, Fiedler, Stokowski, and others (not to say the less noted American conductors who plug them so indefatigably in broadcasts and films), you have been hearing no more than the bloodless ghosts of these incomparable dance poems.

Listen instead to the Vienna Philharmonic under Krauss in its "New Year's Concerts" collections—and not only to the familiar melodies of *Tales from the Vienna Woods* (heard here in full native dress, with the fascinating original zither solos), but also to the exotically stirring *Egyptian March*, and a whole grab-bag of perky polkas, many of which are by Johann's scarcely less talented brother Josef.

On a larger scale and even more appetizingly rich in melodic sweetness, rhythmic spice, and *Gemütlichkeit* is the complete Viennese *Fledermaus*, certainly one of the most ingratiating introductions to the kaleidoscopic realm of opera on records, and perhaps the most ingratiating of all. But, again, don't be hornswoggled into accepting substitutes for the real McCoy; the American versions with old or new English texts, no matter how famous their casts or the seeming advantages of hearing the words in your own language, capture only a negligible fraction of the music's authentic enticement.

If you're instinctively more vocal- than instrument-minded (a significant distinction I'll discuss later on), other effective steppingstones well might be the thrillingly voiced English song recitals by Kathleen Ferrier; certainly the haunting sorcery of Villa-Lobos's *Bachianas Brasileiras* No. 5 as sung by Bidú Sayão; and another kind of magically distilled nostalgia in the radiantly arching choral melody of Bach's *Jesu, Joy of Man's Desiring* (from Cantata 147), with its gravely frolicsome oboe ornamentations—a particularly happy choice if you've heard this music before only in piano or orchestral transcriptions.

For the more strongly orchestral-minded, Schubert's lovely little Fifth and Bizet's Schubertian C major are two of the most immediately appealing symphonies I can recommend. And Britten's *Young Person's Guide to the Orchestra* combines a magnificent Purcell tune with exciting, not too "modern" variations, as well as serving as an exceptionally clear descriptive map or Baedeker for your first investigations into the various instruments and "choirs" that go to make up a full symphony orchestra.

There will be more steppingstone suggestions later, but I can't break off this preliminary sampling without

getting in three of the gold-star works that always will
have essential niches in my own basic record library.
They are all by Handel: the red beef and strong brandy of
his *Water Music* (first perhaps in the Harty abridgment, but
eventually in the complete edition), the dramatic power
and pomp of his Concerto for Orchestra in D, and—perhaps
best of all—Sir Thomas Beecham's superbly eloquent arrangement and performance of *The Faithful Shepherd* suite.

❖❖❖❖❖❖❖

4. The "Good-Tune" Touchstone

> *And the tunes that mean so much to you alone ...*
> *I can rip your very heartstrings out with those.*
> —KIPLING: *The Song of the Banjo*

LISTENERS who insist on highly individualized approaches
to great music undoubtedly are (for better or worse) in the
minority. In any case, there are obvious limitations on
the available supply of completely reliable steppingstones
of either the personal-discovery or the bandwagon types.
Sooner or later every novice has to graduate from being
spoonfed on guaranteed digestibles and learn both to develop and to exercise his own powers of choice.

Even at this stage you have much more to work with
than when all serious music was completely new to you.
If you stop to reconsider the works you know already, it's
apparent that they are each characterized by at least one
distinctive quality, some of them by several, and that these
different qualities exert markedly different kinds of appeal.
Let's look at these qualities more closely—not only to aid
you in their identification and recognition, but also to decide just how and why they vary so notably (for you) in
their attractiveness.

In elementary music-education, music is traditionally
dissected into its prime components. *Melody* is the first of

these (which surprises the ignoramus only in its implication that there are others), but *rhythm* and *harmony* are vitally important too. Somewhat grudgingly, it is conceded that there's another significant if mysterious element known variously as *timbre* or *tone-color*. And of course there always is *form* in addition, though it's seldom clear (and not only to novices) whether this is an element in itself or a kind of box or mold into which the actual elements are poured to set in proper shape.

Yet it should be obvious to any listener who brings a grain of common sense to thinking about what he hears that any rigid segregation of music's "elements" is a dangerously artificial procedure, except when confined exclusively to analytical study. Can we ever have a melody without at the same time having some kind of rhythm, usually with one or more at least implied harmonies in addition? Doesn't even the simplest melody have some kind of mood-color in itself, to say nothing of the external coloring given it by the voice or instrument through which it comes to life? And isn't even the simplest of forms—a short song, say—actually a quite complex, even if minute *organism*, based on inextricably blended and interacting melodic, rhythmic, coloristic, and structural principles?

Reason alone should confirm these doubts even for the great tunes mentioned in Chapter ii. And among the larger works suggested so far, it is obvious that none could exist except as an organic whole. Trying to imagine what they'd removed is like picturing the grin on the face of the Cheshire cat after both cat and face have vanished.

All this, however, is not to deny the importance of such factors as basic elementary principles in music or of the ability to distinguish them as vital for full musical enjoyment. What I want to warn the novice listener against is settling too early on an arbitrary and far too restricted definition of any of these elements in isolation, and particularly his dangerous tendency to squeeze what should be a germinal melodic principle into the narrow confines of a "good tune." All tunes are melodies, of course, but not all melodies (let alone the melodic principle itself) can be summed up as tunes—at least in the common-sense definition of "an air any child can whistle, sing, or follow."

To avoid misconceptions, then, let us just say that the melodic principle in general unquestionably exerts one of the strongest—perhaps the basic—attractions for all kinds of listeners. In its simplest form—a good tune that anyone can whistle or follow—it probably is the prime attraction for very young, untrained, and inexperienced listeners. Nevertheless, I hope to convince you that the exclusive search for good tunes seriously limits your musical growth.

First, any good tune is so perfectly complete in itself that it seldom can lead anywhere except to self-repetition. Next, concentration on the tunes in larger works tends to isolate a few admired but brief moments from the longer stretches when whatever is going on fails to hold the listener's interest as he waits impatiently for the re-appearance of the "essential" tune (much, indeed, as a child carefully picks the raisins out of a piece of cake and blandly throws the rest away). And, perhaps most danger-ous of all, good tunes tend to become encrusted (like grains of sand in oysters) with a pearly coating of emotional associations, which greatly enhance their poignance, but which, because they are primarily non-musical in charac-ter, more often distract than aid the listener's concen-trated attention on purely musical factors.

To convince yourself of the disadvantages, as well as the advantages, of great tunes, go back to as many familiar works as you can. Listen closely to the moments of special tunefulness, but attentively compare these with every-thing else that goes into the making of the whole piece or work. Or try some of the following examples, familiar or unfamiliar, forgetting for the moment any precon-ceived notions you may have about the music's abstract greatness or lightness:

Auber's *Fra Divaolo* and other overtures, Chopin's Etude No. 3, Dvořák's Serenade for strings, Elgar's *Pomp and Circumstance* marches, Grainger's setting of the folksong

Early One Morning, Grieg's *Norwegian Dances*, Luigini's *Ballet Egyptien*, the Intermezzo from Mascagni's *Cavalleria rusticana*, Rubinstein's *Kamenoi Ostrov*, Sibelius's *Finlandia* and *Valse triste*, Suk's and Tchaikovsky's serenades for strings.

I think that several points of interest are likely to emerge from such a tune-fest once you begin to ponder what you've been hearing. One is that even the shorter, most self-contained tunes have at least some additional, "contrasting" materials, while in the larger works there usually are one or more contrasting sections. Obviously, even the tune comprises more than a single melodic idea, even though the others are kept subsidiary and perhaps used mainly to point up the effectiveness of the dominant tune-germ. And, plainly, in any piece of sustained length, no one tune can be extended too far; other (usually contrasting) materials have to be introduced, some of which may be distinctive tunes themselves, but equally well may be quite different kinds of either "filler" or functionally more independent music.

Another noteworthy point is that while some of the main tunes are so obvious that after hearing (even for the first time) the opening phrases, you probably can complete them yourself. Others take more surprising turns that you hardly could have anticipated. And if you do enough listening, you'll soon find that it is tunes of the latter type that better retain their freshness after frequent repetition.

The third and perhaps most curious point is the novice's disconcerting discovery that most of his favorite tunes seem to be considered commonplace, if not "cheap," by many more experienced listeners and writers on music. More discouragingly still, these "superior" friends and authorities apparently find their richest musical enjoyment in larger works where he (poor fellow!) often is unable to disentangle a bewildering welter of sound into any tunes he can follow, let alone retain.

But by this time perhaps you have the clue to this last puzzle. Its mystery begins to evaporate once you start thinking about melodic principles rather than tunes; it disappears entirely when you fully realize that melodiousness is defined and evalued by every listener on the basis of his own standards and experience. Where the novice's great limitation is his tendency to regard anything strange with distaste, if not fear, that of the sophisticate is to regard the overfamiliar with condescension or actual contempt.

This may sound pretty disheartening, but fortunately the majority of listeners seldom, or for long, find themselves in such extremities. Even the novice, originally limited to the recognition of "good tunes," soon develops the capacity of finding melodic significance in more complex materials and subtler forms. Some of his early favorites, unless they possess exceptional strength, may then seem to lose their initial force. But, in compensation, he discovers that generally the larger and more complex a musical work is, the longer it takes him to exhaust its interest. The practical problem, then, is how best to shift your main musical interests from relatively short, simple, and tuneful pieces to those of greater length and complexity. Or, put another way, how best to expand and deepen your individual conception of melodiousness.

The straightforward search for good tunes, however rewarding it may be at first, usually leads eventually to a dead end. The larger world of musical enjoyment opens up only when you change your objective and make use of your developed notion of tunefulness as a kind of *touchstone* for discovering the essential melodic principle however and wherever it may appear. The goal no longer is a good tune itself, but the lift, charm, and eloquence that are the basic sources of such a tune's appeal.

One of the best fields in which to begin this "good-tune touchstone" exploration is that of *variations*, for in such works the composer helps you out by clearly stating the tune he is using as a theme, and then proceeding to develop not only the tune itself, but also the basic melodic ideas it contains—ideas that also are expressible in a wide variety of forms and treatments.

Several examples (by Brahms, Britten, Franck, and Rachmaninoff) have been mentioned earlier. Several other works already suggested contain sections or movements either in variation form or in that of the not dissimilar *rondo* (where repetitions of a main theme, sometimes varied itself, are interspersed with contrasting "episodes"). In addition to these, a good batch of introductory variations might include:

Arensky's *Variations on a Theme by Tchaikovsky*, Beethoven's cello variations on Mozart themes, Dohnányi's *Variations on a Nursery Tune*, Haydn's "Emperor" Quartet, Rimsky-Korsakov's and others' *Tati-Tati* (variations on *Chopsticks*), Schubert's *"Forellen"* Quintet, and the Theme and Variations from Tchaikovky's third Orchestral Suite.

But of course you don't have to stick exclusively to what are entitled "variations." In addition to the variation and rondo movements in symphonies and other larger works, there is wealth of music under other names (fantasias, rhapsodies, etc.) which makes use of easily recognizable "good tunes" in a variety of combinations, embroideries, and developments—among which even the novice should have little difficulty in following the working-out of the basic melodic materials.

Try, for example: Anderson's *Irish* suite, Bruch's *Scottish Fantasy*, Chávez's setting of the Mexican song *La Paloma Azul*, the first movement of Dvořák's unnumbered Symphony in E flat, Enesco's *Romanian Rhapsody* No. 1, Ravel's *La Valse*, Schumann's *Carnaval*, and Weinberger's *Schwanda* Polka and Fugue.

And if at this stage you have the courage to explore further, try listening to some similar works, in which neither the theme nor the working-out may always be as readily apprehensible, but which also can be clarified by patient use of the melodic principle's open-sesame: Bach's "Goldberg" Variations, Franck's Prelude, Choral, and Fugue, Haydn's Variations in F minor, d'Indy's Symphony on a French Mountain Air, Mendelssohn's *Variations sérieuses*, Reger's *Variations on a Theme by Mozart*, and, whatever else you try, the grave, profoundly moving Vaughan Williams *Fantasia on a Theme by Tallis*.

If you've been able to shift the focus of your primary attention from tunes to melodic ideas, you may have found yourself listening with at least interest, if not complete comfort, to those traditional *bêtes noires* of the novice— *fugues*. And if you've paid close attention, perhaps you have discovered for yourself that essentially a fugue isn't too different from a theme with variations. The distinction (in part) is that here the theme is less a tune than a melodic idea, and the working-out usually is a concise *development* of that idea rather than a series of variations of the embroidery or ornamentation type.

Besides the fugues included in the Franck and Reger works mentioned immediately above (and those by Britten, Weinberger, and others cited earlier), other good introductory examples are Bach's "Little" Fugue in G minor and the three Münchinger string-orchestral transcriptions of Bach fugues on London LL 526. Don't be surprised if you find the last of these somewhat enigmatic, as well as strangely moving. This Ricercare in Six Parts from the *Muscial Offering* is one of the greatest works of all music in fugal style and one of those rare works of any type which can be heard and studied for years without ever exhausting the power of its incomparably thrilling drama.

But whether or not you're up to tackling (just yet) what may seem like pretty difficult music, you now can turn back to use your new good-tune touchstone on many other, "easier" works. With it in hand you can make far more enlightened first approaches to entirely unfamiliar music, or far more revelatory reappraisals of music you've heard before, but for which you previously lacked the alchemical gift of transmitting "filler" passages into the pure gold of melodiousness.

❖❖❖❖❖❖❖

5. The Dynamic Stimulus

> *From the beginning of organic existence,*
> *{man's} consciousness has been induced, ex-*
> *panded, trained in the lines of his sensitive-*
> *ness; and the rise of his faculties from a*
> *lower power to a higher, or from a narrower*
> *to a wider field may be due to the function of*
> *assimilating and storing outside force or*
> *forces.*
> —*The Education of Henry Adams*

In a good many years of thought and study, I've managed to capture only one significant insight into my own and other's musical growth-patterns. Like most vital truisms, it is deceptively obvious: the direction of all natural, healthy growth invariably lies *with the grain* of the individual listener's temperament.

Many novices have at least a subconscious inkling of this truth. One of their first discoveries is that they can pragmatically guarantee musical pleasure by listening only to works they like. Usually it isn't until much later that they're ready to face up to the larger question of *why* they enjoy one work and fail to enjoy another. As long as they rely on the cliché justification of taste, or tastelessness ("I don't know anything about art, but I know what I like!"), they both under- and over-estimate themselves, as well as rigidly limiting their range of musical activity. Anyone *can* go on indefinitely listening to whatever comes his way and laboriously separating the sheep from the goats by blind "feel," as it were, but this certainly is the hard way to do things. Much otherwise wasted time and effort can be saved by finding out something about music before or while it is heard. But perhaps the most profitable preparatory study is of *oneself*.

Now, one of the fundamental distinctions in human personalities is between the tendency to look outward and the tendency to look inward. Dr. Carl Jung's terms "extravert" and "introvert" have been misunderstood and misused by amateur psychologists who persist in applying one simple label to personalities that actually are a complex bundle of often contradictory (or complementary) qualities. But in most individualities (as in most musical compositions) one of the many component qualities may be—or at least seem to be—outstanding. And such apparently predominant characteristics, while not evidence that can always be taken at its face value, do provide valuable clues to the understanding of the complete personality.

In your own case, if you are primarily an outward-looking, positive, active, gregarious, and extraverted personality, your musical tastes and need will differ widely from those of someone primarily introspective, reserved, "intellectual," and introverted. That doesn't say that you're going to like best music that exhibits comparable qualities of rhythmic animation, bold assurance, and dramatic conflicts. The old "rule of opposites" and the principle of "compensation" often apply here. The man who lives a strenuous, extraverted life may instinctively find needed outlets for the other, hidden aspect of his personality in "restful" introspective music, in much the same way, and perhaps for the same subconscious reasons, that he may marry a demure and placid wife.

On the other hand, many of us who must steel ourselves for harsh contacts with the outer world, who tend to live perhaps too much within ourselves, may find the most satisfactory release of our pent-up tensions in frankly extraverted music—music in which thought gives way almost entirely to sheer action and which seems to provide our whole organisms with both electrifying vitality and catharsis.

Of course, it's foolish to make these attractions of either likes or unlikes absolute and exclusive. But they do indicate two of the main—sometimes alternative, sometimes complementary—highroads to musical enjoyment.

In the last chapter we saw that while melody exerts an almost universal appeal, the melodic principle appears in many forms, and often considerable experience is necessary before it can be appreciated in its subtler manifestations. After listening to a number of good tunes in succession, you probably have found that you felt inexplicably weary. No matter how much you enjoyed what you heard, you began to feel an irresistible urge for something different. Maybe you switched to livelier music; most likely you shut off your phonograph and went out for a vigorous walk or sought some kind of energetic activity.

Such reactions, if you need the reassurance, are wholly normal. For one thing, attentive listening is hard work and, like any kind of intensive effort, must be followeb by a period of relaxation and recuperation. For another, music never has been pure melody. From its beginnings it has been used for dancing, marching, and working, as well as for meditation, worship, and ritual. Music can elevate the soul, but is also can tickle the toes. And just because it reaches so directly to the brain-cells and nerves that initiate and control muscular activity, it is an unparalleled stimulant of both actual physical movement and (even more significantly) the *sense* of motion.

Let's test this power of dynamic stimulus, first in smaller works that exemplify musical *action* in its most obvious forms, then progressing gradually through longer, more varied, and more complex examples. Some earlier suggestions may be repeated, but now try to approach these works (or others already familiar) from a new angle. Instead of concentrating on tunes, or even melodic principles, focus your sharpest attention on their *dynamic* qualities, not only the basic beat, but also the counter-rhythms, the fast-slow and loud-soft contrasts, the ways in which a sense of momentum is built up, sustained, and finally brought to a conclusive stop.

Begin with some simple marches, those by Sousa, say, and Halvorsen's *March of the Boyards*, Pierné's *March of the Little Lead Soldiers*, Schubert's *March Militaire*, and the little march from Tchaikovsky's *Nutcracker Suite*. Then go on to larger works, say the Funeral March from Beethoven's Third ("*Eroica*") symphony, Berlioz's *Rakóczy March* (*La*

Damnation de Faust) and "March to the Scaffold" (*Symphonie fantastique*), Rimsky-Korsakov's "Bridal Cortège" (*Le Coq d'or*), Tchaikovsky's *Marche slave* and the march-scherzo from his Sixth ("*Pathétique*") Symphony.

To shift from marches to dances, the Strauss (Johann and Josef) polkas make ideal springboards, as do the Brahms *Hungarian Dances* and the even jauntier, more warmly vital *Slavonic Dances* by Dvořák. Then try Smetana's lusty polka and furiant from *The Bartered Bride*, his vivacious *Bohemian Dances*, and the infectiously intoxicating, whirling "Girls' Dance" from Borodin's *Prince Igor*. For still more exuberant and violently energetic dance music, go on to Copland's *El Salón México*, the "Russian Sailors' Dance" from Glière's *Red Poppy*, the "Dagger Dance" from Khachaturian's *Gayne* (if the juke boxes haven't spoiled it for you!), Kodály's *Dances from Galanta*, the "Dance of the Tumblers" from Rimsky-Korsakov's *Snow Maiden*, "Salome's Dance" from Richard Strauss's *Salome*, and of course the supremely breath-taking final dances from the Borodin *Prince Igor* and Ravel *Daphnis et Chloë* ballets.

After such workouts as these, you'll have to rest up to get your wind back. But when you're rested, experiment with less strenuous examples of dynamism. Some of these may seem almost too ethereal for the term to apply—that is, until you begin to realize that vehemence and animation aren't synonymous, that there is a poetry of gentler motion, and that buoyancy and grace may be as stimulating as raw energy.

Chopin's mazurkas (aptly called "dances of the soul") are fine to start with, as are his less fanciful, more elegant waltzes (which, someone once quipped, must have been written to be danced by countesses only). Or try the *Spanish Dances* by Granados, that by Falla from *La Vida Breve*, and some of the others in Jorda's admirable disc-collection. Also Berlioz's feather-light "Dance of the Sylphs" and "Minuet of the Will-o'-the-Wisps" (*La Damnation de Faust*), the poetic *Habanera* by Chabrier and *Pièce en forme d'un habanera* by Ravel, Copland's easy-shuffling "Celebration

Dance" (*Billy the Kid*), and the daintily stepping "*Passo a sei*" from Rossini's *Guglielmo Tell*.

From such relatively small-scale works, it's an easy sliding dance-step to complete ballets brimming with more varied examples of music that is both toe-tickling and heart-lifting. Two of the most zestful are the Boccherini-Françaix *School of Dancing* and the Scarlatti-Tommasini *Good-Humored Ladies*. From there you can go on to Falla's *El Amor Brujo* and *Three-Cornered Hat*, Lecocq's *Mlle Angot*, the Offenbach-Rosenthal *Gaîté parisienne*, the Strauss-Dorati *Graduation Ball*, Stravinsky's *Firebird* and *Petrouchka*, and of course Tchaikovsky's *Sleeping Beauty* and *Swan Lake*.

But it isn't necessary to look for dynamic attractions in the march and dance repertories exclusively. While most "action" music makes use of dance or march elements, these may appear under diverse names in many metamorphoses. The scherzos and finales of many standard concertos and symphonies provide excellent examples. For other, relatively familiar or easy, try the collection discs of Auber, Berlioz, and Rossini overtures, Chabrier's *España*, Dukas's *L'Apprenti sorcier*, Debussy's *Fêtes* (Nocturne No. 2), the scherzos from Mendelssohn's *Midsummer Night's Dream* and Octet, Ravel's *Boléro*, the "Comedians' Scene" from Smetana's *Bartered Bride*, Johann Strauss's *Perpetuum Mobile*, and the "Ride of the Valkyries" from Wagner's *Walküre*.

For less familiar (hence, perhaps even more piquant) musical stimulants, try Albéniz's *Ibéria*, Bartók's Romanian and Bulgarian dances, Elgar's *Cockaigne* Overture, Gershwin's *Variations on "I've Got Rhythm*," Kabalevsky's *The Comedians*, Kodály's *Háry János* suite, Poulenc's *Mouvements perpetuels*, Prokofiev's *Lieutenant Kije* suite, Shostakovich's *L'Âge d'or* polka, and Stravinsky's two suites for small orchestra.

From these it shouldn't be hard to go back or forward to almost innumerable other works that apparently have nothing to do with dancing or marching, but which convey a not dissimilar sense of controlled energy, and often fill one with an even more profound feeling of invigoration: the

Amen Chorus from Handel's *Messiah*, for example, Bach's toccatas and fugues (including, but not confined to, the most famous one in D minor), the last movement of Schubert's mighty C major Symphony, Siegfried's "Rhine Journey" and "Death Music" from Wagner's *Götterdämmerung*, and perhaps the complete Act III of his *Meistersinger*.

You'll find that listening to such vigorous music often is accompanied by actual rises in your blood pressure and pulse rate. For much of music's familiar invigoration results from the fact that it simulates the energy-supplying effects of sugar, or even the at first stimulating and later intoxicating effects of alcohol.

We mustn't forget that "tone" is a word of more than musical meaning. It also has a physiological definition— "the degree of firmness or tension proper to organs or tissues of the body in a strong and healthy condition."

"Toning-up" your system through music is achieved in the simplest fashion, of course, by lively marches and dances. But just as the melodic principle can be expanded far beyond the limits of a good tune, the principle of rhythmic animation can be developed into complex interplays of stressed and relaxed tensions. In such forms you no longer may be able to tap out simple rhythmic pulses (any more than you can whistle or sing certain complex melodies), but your are nonetheless conscious of inner feelings of motion, acceleration, and momentum.

Indeed, there are some works (by Bach, Handel, and certain modern composers, in particular) which, as you've probably discovered for yourself by this time, can impress their listeners with the sense of immense force and high-speed but controlled motion that you feel so profoundly when you stand beside the almost silently whirring dynamos of an electric-power station. And such works, like the dynamos themselves, well may be among mankind's most valuable sources of replenishment for our prodigal expenditures of energy.

6. Escape to Dream Worlds

. . . Sounds and sweet airs, that give delight and hurt not.
Sometimes a thousand twangling instruments
Will hum about mine ears, and sometime voices
That, if I then had waked after long sleep,
Will make me sleep again: and then, in dreaming,
The clouds methought would open and show riches
Ready to drop upon me, that, when I waked,
I cried to dream again.

—SHAKESPEARE: *The Tempest*

THE STRAINS and stresses of modern life, which steadily
multiply the demand for alcohol, Benzedrine, and other
stimulants, also account for a phenomenal increase in the
consumption of sedatives, from aspirin to sleeping-pills. Yet
even the most potent drugs fall far short of meeting the
contemporary hunger for both invigoration and relaxation.
Besides being dangerous and expensive, they become pro-
gressively shorter-lived in their effectiveness. The safest,
cheapest, and most reliable prescription for our un- and
dis-satisfactions still is what old-time doctors recommended
as a "change of scenery" or what a present-day psychiatrist
might term the "escape-valves" of travel, sports, and other
kinds of entertainment.

Yet though the demand for "escapist" entertainment has
become both widespread and insatiable, it still is fiercely
denounced as a kind of reprehensible drug-addiction. And
the actual mass-favored escape vehicles themselves draw
even fiercer fire for their lamentable lack of "serious"
artistic worth.

Reprehensible or not, the need itself has become a basic
one. If shoddy entertainment often is chosen to meet it,
that well may be only because nothing better is known to be
available. In any case, the urge to "escape" doesn't necessarily imply a cowardly or lazy reluctance to "face reality."
Even purists and highbrows, who scorn recourse to crude
stimulants and opiates, who contemptuously disdain pop-

ular comic-books, broadcast, film, and television "shows," themselves require a good night's sleep after a busy day, a vacation to quiet or exotic resorts after a year's work in the city, and regular access to books, plays, and music that provide the heaven-sent relief of "taking one out of oneself."

In these pages we'll have to abandon the larger part of escapist musical entertainment (so-called popular songs, dance and background music) to the worried attention of psychologists and educators. But as the kinds of music we are dealing with here are also widely used—and useful— in the momentary escape to dream worlds, we can't afford to ignore this phenomenon. Indeed, it may be well worth our while to investigate the possible exploitation of so natural and powerful a human tendency as a means of both enhancing our over-all musical enjoyment and expanding our musical horizons.

Examined first from our present point of view of temperamental slants or biases, the appeal of "escape" music plainly isn't confined to either outward- or inward-looking personalities. Its own characteristics may resemble those of the predominantly dynamic works just discussed, or those frequently occurring in the more introspective works we will turn to in the next chapter. But if "escape" works make use, as do others, of all the basic musical qualities, the dominant, distinctive ones surely are *color* and *atmosphere*.

Unfortunately, these terms are extremely loose, and the former in particular is often misunderstood. In general, these are less qualities in themselves than special qualifications of simpler and more easily identified musical elements, particularly harmonic textures and the tone-timbres employed in scoring and performance. Whatever the means used, the decisive result is to produce in the listener impressions of evocative poetry, "strange" fascination, or the persuasive nostalgia of "old, unhappy, far-off things, and battles long ago."

"Persuasive" probably is the key word for whatever it is that gives some music its inexplicable power to bewitch its listeners into Coleridge's "willing suspension of disbelief."

One particularly striking exploitation of these qualities is the frank plagiarizing, by Tin-Pan Alley and Hollywood songsmiths, of "serious" romantic and impressionistic composers' most colorful melodic turns and harmonic and timbre schemes. Sometimes this is done crudely, sometimes with extraordinary ingenuity, but the purpose always is to enrich the "mood effectiveness" of the commercial productions, and in general the practice has been so successful that both formal and informal music-education eventually must reckon with its far-reaching results.

For, on one hand, novice listeners gradually have become indoctrinated in many of the idioms and devices that formerly made most impressionistic and "modern" art music so forbiddingly alien on first hearing. On the other, unfortunately, such music's essential magic is weakened and diluted as it loses its "strangeness." The more obvious examples of musical exoticism, like the most obvious tunes, quickly lose their original bloom with overfamiliarity.

It largely depends, then, on your previous experience whether you are fascinated or bored by such "easy" examples of picturesque tone-painting and poetry as Chopin's *Berceuse* and nocturnes, Grofé's *Grand Canyon* suite, Humperdinck's *Hänsel und Gretel* "Dream Pantomime," Ippolitov-Ivanov's *Caucasian Sketches*, MacDowell's *Woodland Sketches* and *Sea Pieces*, Mussorgsky's *Night on Bald Mountain*, Wagner's *Siegfried* "*Waldweben*" and *Walküre* "magic-fire scene," and the overtures to Weber's *Oberon* and *Der Freischütz*.

But from these it is an easy step to other bits of scene or mood evocations that are either more subtly colored or more resistant to plagiarists' despoilation: Borodin's *On the Steppes of Central Asia*, Fauré's *Pavane*, Foote's *Night Piece*, Griffes's *Poem* for flute, Mendelssohn's *Midsummer Night's Dream* and *Fingal's Cave* ("Hebrides") overtures, the prelude and entr'acte from Mussorgsky's *Khovanshchina*, Rabaud's *Procession nocturne*, Satie's *Gymnopédies* and *Gnossiennes*, and Sibelius's dark-hued *Swan of Tuonela*.

And we can't go far into such enchanted realms before we reach the domains of music's perhaps greatest tonal sorcerers: Debussy, Ravel, and Delius.

The best introductions to Debussy probably are the *Prélude à l'Après-midi d'un faune*, *Children's Corner* suite, *La Cathédrale engloutie* (*Prélude* No. 10), and *Jardins sous la pluie* (*Estampe* No. 3)—followed by the other *Préludes* and *Estampes*, the *Images* (both those for piano and those for orchestra), *La Demoiselle élue*, and at least some of the songs.

With Ravel, after the popular *Ma Mère l'Oye* and *Pavane*, I suggest going on to the *Jeux d'eaux* and *Miroirs* for piano, the String Quartet in F, and the hauntingly exotic song-cycle *Shéhérazade*.

For Delius (who, perhaps more than any other composer, represents the quintessence of dream-world-escape music for the phonographic listeners of recent years), the first choices are *On Hearing the First Cuckoo in Spring*, *Summer Night on the River*, and the heart-breaking *Walk to the Paradise Gardens;* then (as belated LP releases permit) *Brigg Fair*, the *Dance Rhapsodies*, and *Sea Drift*.

Tone-pictures and tone-poems naturally make up the bulk of the dream-world musical repertory, but it is not confined to them. And, in any case, the type or title of a work is less significant than its atmospheric character.

For further, widely varied examples, try: Berlioz's *Roméo et Juliette*, Bloch's *Schelomo*, Chabrier's *Ode à musique*, Franck's Violin Sonata, Holst's *The Planets*, Milhaud's *La Création du monde*, Rimsky-Korsakov's *Antar* and *Coq d'or* suite (in addition, of course, to the more familiar *Scheherazade*), Sibelius's *En Saga*, Tchaikovsky's *Francesca de Rimini*, Villa-Lobos's *Bachianas Brasileiras* No. 1 (in addition to the better-known No. 5), the prelude, Flower Maidens' scene, and Good Friday Spell from Wagner's *Parsifal*.

In works like these, you will find clear-cut examples of markedly dynamic, extraverted character, some distinctly introspective or introverted, and others that are a blend of both types. But you will find that their characterization depends not only on the music itself, but also on your individual approach to it, and on its particular performance "environment." Played at low level late at night, even the most vigorous works may have a far-away, dreamy effect; played loudly when you yourself are more alert, even the most ethereal of them may make an astonishingly dynamic impact. The best "escape" music is remarkably versatile (or equivocal) in this respect, convincingly supporting Jung's claim that "fantasy" provides the bridge between extraversion and introversion.

In general, however, there is a special "extravert" appeal in music that depicts or evokes exotic places and peoples. Several of these vacation trips (to Spain, Russia, central Asia, etc.) have been suggested earlier, and for further excursion jaunts on the wings of tone, try: Chávez's Mexican Music program, Delius's *Appalachia*, Dvořák's *Slavonic Rhapsodies*, Falla's *Nights in the Gardens of Spain*, Gilbert's *Dance in the Place Congo*, Hovhaness's *Lousadzak*, Ibert's *Escales*, Lambert's *Rio Grande*, Milhaud's *Saudades do Brasil*, Ravel's *Rapsodie espagnole* and *Alborada del gracioso*, Respighi's *Fountains of Rome*, Rimsky-Korsakov's *Capriccio Espagnole* and *Russian Easter* overture, Smetana's *My Country* cycle (which includes the familiar *Moldau*), Richard Strauss's *Aus Italien*, Thomson's *Louisiana Story*, Villa-Lobos's *Uirapurú* and *Chôros* No. 10, and Vaughan Williams's "London" Symphony. And don't miss at least a brief visit to the musical Orient, particularly to hear the sonorous gamelan (gong) orchestras of Bali.

Of course, even the most exotic sights and sounds (whether you travel in the physical world or that of music) filter to your mind through your own eyes and ears. In the full sense of "escape," even endless vacations and world-wide journeying eventually are futile—for you carry yourself and your problems wherever you go.

Nevertheless, music is a more effective aid than any other so-called escapist entertainment in helping you to draw out of yourself momentarily, and also in enabling you to live better with yourself when you return. At its best, "escape" music achieves a dual therapy: taking your mind off your troubles and at the same time supplying you with new strength and insight to cope with these very troubles.

A discussion of such exceptional works properly belongs in the next chapter, but it might be well to attempt your first plunges into deeper waters with music that includes (among other, perhaps even more significant, qualities) enough atmospheric color to make it pertinent here. Anyway, it is high time to turn a bit from "adventures of the senses" to those of the spirit. The latter may involve colorful settings, but they also may take place wholly *within* yourself, or in the dramatic conflict of purely musical—but by no means wholly "abstract"—ideas. What do *you* find in each of the following?

Berlioz's *Harold en Italie* and *Requiem*, Brahms's "Double" Concerto and Clarinet Quintet, Chopin's *Fantaisie*, Couperin's *Tenebræ* services, Debussy's *Pelléas et Mélisande*, Fauré's *Requiem*, Gabrieli's *Canzone*, Haydn's *Mass in Time of War*, Mahler's *Lied von der Erde*, Mozart's *Zauberflöte*, Mussorgsky's *Boris Godunov*, Prokofiev's *Alexander Nevsky*, Smetana's *From My Life*, Schumann's *Fantasie* in C and *Humoreske*, Richard Strauss's *Also sprach Zarathustra* and *Don Quixote*, Stravinsky's *Orpheus*, and Wagner's *Tristan und Isolde*.

7. *The Philosophers' Stone*

> *Hence the singular privilege of this art: to give form to what is naturally inarticulate and express those depths of human nature which can speak no language current in the world.*
> —SANTAYANA: *Reason in Art*

THE foregoing musical approaches are not mutually exclusive, of course, and still less are they our only possible choices. Some of us may want to turn aside occasionally to blaze our own cross-country way or to settle down for the intense cultivation of a single composer's field where we feel inexplicably but securely at home. But most of us have been drawn irresistibly, at one time or another, to join the crowds on the standard-masterpiece bandwagons, to wield the good-tune touchstone in testing new materials for authentic traces of the melodic principle, or to follow the instinctive grain of our own temperament in seeking music that serves as a source either of energy replenishment or of "some sweet oblivious antidote" for the splitting headaches of contemporary life.

Yet no matter how popular and effective any one of these approaches may be, these great, personal highroads to musical enjoyment have a common, inherent limitation. And that lies not in the paths themselves, but in their objective.

Now, to suggest that enjoyment may not be an ideal goal may strike you as prissily puritanical—if not as outright heresy. Certainly it is utterly unreasonable to deny that pleasure is the prime objective of every listener. It may be quibbling to segregate various types of pleasures and rank them in a hierarchy of greater and lesser. But one of the hard lessons we all learn eventually is that the rewards of experience are mixed: hearing more and knowing more don't always mean more enjoyment. Often the contrary is true: after a certain degree of familiarity has been reached, your enjoyment may tend to lose its zest. A favorite piece of music no longer gives us a kick, and we have to turn to something new in search of the old thrill.

This is unimportant early in the game, when an illimitable wealth of still unfamiliar music seems spread out for our grasping, but in the course of time liberally spent in listening, even that treasure-trove begins to seem susceptible of exhaustion. Actually, this danger is illusory, at least within any individual listener's lifetime. But certain rooms in the treasure-house are indeed limited in size and content —and none more than those most easily accessible. Like prospectors who begin by simply picking up nuggets lying on the surface, listeners eventually are faced by the necessity of hard digging if they want to follow and profit by the gold veins that run far underground.

Although this is a hard, disillusioning lesson that everyone must learn, I don't want to exaggerate its difficulties. Some lucky novices may scarcely realize when an intense interest in new experiences leads them around the sharp corner between a more or less passive acceptance of musical pleasure and the active search for it. But unconsciously or deliberately, the turn has to be made. And perhaps nothing prepares us better for that vital step than a redefinition of musical enjoyment, a rephrasing of the question: "What music will give me the most pleasure?" into "What pleasures can I get out of music?"

When you reach this stage, you'll find it immensely helpful to turn back and listen all over again to the music you have come to know best. But this time try to analyze both the music and its effect on you. Just what is it in your favorites that exerts the strongest appeal? Even more important, perhaps, what it is in these or other works that strikes you as less (or even not) enjoyable?

Don't be surprised if no miracles occur and you still like what you liked and dislike what you disliked earlier. Remember that no music (masterpiece or otherwise) fundamentally uncongenial to your individual temperament ever will be wholly satisfactory for you. But if it is an authentic masterpiece, and if you can keep your instinctive biases under reasonable control, the chances are good that you will better recognize those qualities which appeal to other temperaments and which you must at least reluctantly *respect*, even though you can't completely relish or love them yourself.

Another useful type of analysis is distinguishing between works that seem to reveal most or all of their attractions in one or two hearings and those which obviously require many hearings before you can honestly claim that you *know* (whether or not you "like") them. Try sticking awhile longer with some of the latter, especially any that seem to have the power of growing on you. Then ask yourself whether it really is the music that is growing on you. Isn't it perhaps *you* who are growing up to the music?

This is the ideal frame of mind in which to tackle some of the supposedly more difficult works you may have been dodging up to now. You may surprise yourself by finding even these immensely enjoyable at first acquaintance. But whether or not you do is far less significant than developing the ability to find with each rehearing something in them that steadily assumes greater (even if often more puzzling) fascination.

Listen, say, to the Bach *Magnificat*—a particularly apt choice if you've known Bach until now only in "arrangements," and if you hesitate to plunge into the almost infinite depths of his great B minor Mass and Passions. The *Magnificat* is a relatively short work, yet it contains something close to the very quintessence of Bach's incomparable art, a concise revelation of the matchless eloquence and titanic driving force that are spread at greater length in the larger works.

Then go back to the six-part Ricercare mentioned in Chapter iv. This time, however, after hearing it once or twice by itself, listen to the entire *Musical Offering* of which it is crown and climax. Here is—seemingly—none of the dramatic excitement of the *Magnificat*. But listen again and again until you realize that beneath the smooth flow of this music is drama of quite another sort—the drama of pure ideas, of philosophy, of the implacable sweep of human destiny toward an inevitable but unfeared heroic fate. Or read whatever else you want into it. The vital thing is that you at least are aware of *meaning* of some kind—and that you are strangely moved by it.

And after you're all through, stop and ponder both the experience you've just had and what the experience itself has meant to you. Was it enjoyment? If so, didn't it differ very considerably in *kind*, rather than merely in degree, from most musical pleasure that you've known before?

This search for the richer satisfactions rather than the surface delights of musical enjoyment could be continued

almost indefinitely in the works of Bach alone. You well
may want to! But of course even Bach cannot satisfy everybody all the time, or some unfortunates even part of the
time. In any case, there are other great artists whose works
encompass not only the more familiar musical attractions,
but also—and even more richly—the endlessly absorbing
fascination of the human comedy of man wrestling with
his own ideas, of man valiantly attempting to resolve the
prickly contradictions of both his own mind and his outer
world.

For myself, I'd turn next to Handel and Mozart, say the
twelve Opus 6 *Concerti grossi* by the former, probably the
string quintets K.515, K.516, and K.593 and the symphonies K.504 and K.550 by the latter. On one level, all these
are prodigally rich in warmly outspoken melody, throbbing
with rhythmic vitality, and brightly or darkly—but always
imaginatively—colored. Such topmost attractions alone are
enough to hold and delight your attention through many
hearings. But as they become familiar, you surely can't fail
to realize the profounder depths beneath these gleaming
surfaces, depths of passion that can be only surmised, not
apprehended, by the conscious mind.

Many listeners find comparable wonders in Beethoven,
where there are perhaps even clearer implications of the
heroic struggles of man against himself and his fate. Listen
to the Ninth Symphony, of course, but also to the piano
sonatas, Opp. 106, 109, 110, and 111, the "Diabelli" Variations, and the "last" quartets, especially Op. 132 (with
its famed slow movement in the Lydian mode) and Op. 131
with—or separate from—the *Grosse Fuge* that was its original
finale.

On the old score of temperamental bias (the basis of most
individual philosophies and aesthetic standards), I must
confess here that I'm unable to share completely the ecstatic
reverence in which Beethoven's last works are held by many
if not most experienced listeners. I don't think I'm insensitive to their grandeur and poignance, but what undoubtedly is an irrational stubbornness in my own receptivity

prevents my being swept off my feet. As I've suggested before, however, any such idiosyncrasies of taste shouldn't disturb us too much. Often they disappear in the course of our musical and philosophical growth; when they remain as permanent quirks, they must be accepted as such.

In either case, they're usually complemented by other positive quirks that lead one to find special merits in other, less widely esteemed music. I'm certainly not alone or even exceptional in my susceptibility to the imaginative freshness and daring of the Purcell fantasias, for example, but it's doubtful whether their strange power is as potent for at least the majority of listeners. Again it doesn't really matter, except to ourselves, so long as we stretch to its utmost the elasticity of our own sensibilities—in whatever direction it is most naturally extensible.

Far too many listeners, I suspect, make the costly mistake of setting some arbitrary boundary for themselves, beyond which they fear they will be lost or out of their depth. How can you know what your safe depths are, or the limits of your sustaining powers, until you have developed and tested them? How can you be sure that some piece of music that you found hopelessly impenetrable a year or more ago won't now yield to your matured abilities of concentration and pertinacity?

With so-called "modernistic" music, in particular, it is far too easy to give up simply because you're puzzled or affronted at first by the harshness of a language that seems alien and ugly to you. Perhaps it appears ugly only because it is alien.

Discover for yourself whether such apparently formidable works as Bartók's Concerto for Orchestra and Stravinsky's *Symphonie de psaumes*, for example, don't lose much of their terrors with closer acquaintance. And making that closer acquaintance may be eased immeasurably if you prepare yourself in advance by becoming familiar with some of the "easier" works by these and other contemporary composers. You've already found that what seemed at first like the "dry" counterpoint of Bach couldn't long conceal the turmoils and resolutions of soul-shaking drama, that what once seemed like the facile songfulness of Handel and Mozart was but the surface glitter of oceans whose lower depths were swept by tides of supreme passion.

If you only give Bartók and Stravinsky a fair chance to speak both for themselves and to you, you also may find profundity and tenderness of very human and very moving expression beneath their seemingly harsh acerbities.

But again, whether you succeed in these particular instances, or at this particular stage of your musical growth, is of comparatively slight significance. Once you have expanded your personal definition of musical enjoyment, new perspectives and panoramas open up on every side. Once you have learned to prize music that offers a challenge to your sense of pleasure rather than immediate gratification of it, you have at last grown (perhaps laboriously, perhaps in a flash) out of your musical childhood and adolescence into maturity.

Whatever your coming of age may have cost you in growing-pains, your new and sharpened sensibilities, your broader, more discerning, and more tolerant outlook are well worth any cost. For it is these that can serve you as a kind of magical divining rod which (far more effectively than the good-tune touchstone alone) infallibly locates and identifies the most deeply buried musical treasures. In these you now have a new, personal philosophers' stone that can miraculously transmute what may seem at first like the basest of tonal slag into the purest gold.

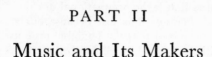

PART II

Music and Its Makers

8. Backgrounds for Listening

> *The charm of history and its enigmatic lesson*
> *consist in the fact that, from age to age,*
> *nothing changes and yet everything is com-*
> *pletely different.*
> —ALDOUS HUXLEY: *The Devils of Loudon*

ABOUT the time a childish craving for immediate enjoyment develops into the maturer urge for more profound and lasting rewards, another major landmark is reached in many listeners' musical growth. It, too, signalizes a fundamental change in attitude, usually first revealed as a sense of *un*-satisfaction with the haphazard shape and restricted extent of one's previous musical experience.

It is at this stage that many of us suddenly become active concert- and opera-goers, sign up for "appreciation" courses, or plunge into the enormous literature "on" music. Our record-buying, too, is stepped up, usually taking a more systematic turn as we begin planning a more "comprehensive" library—one we hope eventually will include representative examples of all major composers, periods, and styles.

This desire for background knowledge and catholic record collections is an admirable token of musical adulthood —at least if you conveniently ignore any contributing elements that are rooted in uneasy feelings of "inferiority," in the vanity of "keeping up with the Joneses" in music as in everything else, and in the cancerous growth of sheer acquisitiveness that is the occupational disease of collectors of any kind. Perhaps it is just because our subconscious motives are so mixed that the laudable urge itself often is satisfied with superficial fulfillment or tends to peter out entirely as time goes on and inevitable difficulties crop up.

These difficulties actually aren't excessive. Anyone seriously determined to surmount them can do so. But few adult non-professional listeners have the time and sustained drive that are demanded. A few energetic people succeed, the lazy ones quit, and the majority are content to make sporadic feeble efforts, usually confined to occasional disc purchases of highly reputed but unfamiliar music, desultory reading, and regular resolutions to buckle down to real study—someday soon.

Unluckily, even the spotty, quite superficial bits of information we accumulate in such cursory listening and reading provide a comfortable, even if synthetic, feeling of being "in the know." Self-delusion is so convenient that few of us ever stop to remember the gullible willingness of human nature (as shrewdly noted by Wolfgang Köhler) "to be soothed and satisfied whenever a problem instead of being solved, has merely been located somewhere."

But why kid yourself along? If you have no genuine intention of intensive music study, forget your ambitious dreams and settle down to whatever gradual accumulation of useful knowledge is practicable for you—particularly in the way of background information on the music you currently take most interest in. Whenever you run across some unfamiliar term or name or statement in LP disc-jacket annotations or record reviews, say, look it up for further details. Until and if you decide really to study more deeply, a large music encyclopedia is hardly essential. A little dictionary of musical terms will be of considerable help in the beginning, if only for definitions and pronunciations, but better still is such a convenient, well-illustrated, one-volume reference work, aimed specifically at the general listener, such as Percy Scholes's *Oxford Companion to Music*.

Collections of program notes, composers' biographies and letters, even some of the more reputable "appreciation" books, undoubtedly will add something to your general musical knowledge. It is seldom, however, that all their "facts" are completely reliable. Their value usually is less informational than stimulative, keeping your musical interests stirred up and encouraging you to hear for yourself the works so enticingly described by others.

Indeed, all writing *about* music is at best an indirect approach to the music itself, which can be truly known only in direct, attentive hearing and re-hearing. Except as a provocation to listening, reading's great value is in helping you to organize your thinking about music *after* you have heard it (though not necessarily in the same pattern as the writer suggests). Perhaps its most valuable function is in guiding your general musical *orientation*—that is, in aiding you to see the entire repertory in larger perspective, to "place" individual composers and works in the over-all picture, and to grasp their relationships with other composers and works.

Valuable as strictly technical and æsthetic study may be, fascinating as biographical and programmatic details often are, the essential background knowledge for the average listener is a working grasp of music *history*—not, of course, as a dreary catalogue of events and dates, but as the living pattern of the art over the ages.

Now, there are innumerable histories of music, written for many purposes and from widely diverse points of view. Some deal primarily with changing forms and media of expression, some with the stylistic idioms of the musical language itself. Many of them are concerned mainly with the achievements of composers, individually or in "schools," and some, especially in recent years, endeavor to correlate musical activities with those in the other arts, perhaps even with broader sociological, political, and philosophical trends.

But neither the detailed fabric nor the profounder implications of history can have much point before you have
learned to discern the basic, underlying structure. Perhaps
the best pragmatic approach is a bare preliminary tracing
of the main outlines, to be eked out by whatever background knowledge you already possess, and of course specifically illustrated, wherever possible, by music you already
know or are able to hear.

So sketchy a once-over as that traced in the next six
chapters obviously isn't music history itself, even in cap-
sule. I offer it only as an introduction to general periods,
trends, and outstanding names—not as a substitute for
more detailed and better-integrated knowledge. Even so,
I hope that it can provide a kind of framework for assem-
bling in more meaningful order the materials already in
your possession. In particular, it may be helpful in indicating just where the music you now know fits into the
larger scheme of things, and in roughly mapping tonal
territories still largely or entirely foreign to your direct
musical experience.

This, like every view of history, is strongly colored by
its writer's own background and prejudices, and always
should be taken as a provocation to your own thinking
rather than as any objective "truth." But I hope that there
may be enough here, even in what seems or is controversial,
to stimulate your further reading both in over-all music
history[1] and in that of special periods.

The major advantages of *some* kind of historical perspective generally are plain enough even to the novice.
What is much less apparent is the danger of *mis*-reading

---

[1] Out of the wealth of available literature, I'd like to recommend two
fine short histories, Curt Sachs's *Our Musical Heritage* and Alfred Einstein's *A Short History of Music*, and the outstanding, more extensive,
but still one-volume work, Paul Henry Lang's *Music in Western Civilization*. And if you begin to read extensively in this eternally fascinating
field, W. D. Allen's *Philosophies of Music History* provides a superb basis
for better understanding and reconciling the diverse and often bluntly
contradictory points of view of historians themselves.

history: the unthinking acceptance of superficial or falla-
cious notions (or any others, for that matter) as absolute
verities rather than fictions and hypotheses that must be
subjected to the tests of time and experience. The following chapters, like any more extensive survey, need to be
prefaced by several emphatic warnings. For you run a
very real risk of falling victim to some of the major de-
lusions than entrap all historical thinking, but perhaps
nowhere more insidiously than in the field of music.

The worst of these (for which Darwin is usually blamed,
but his misinterpreters would be more justly) is the delusion
of "straight-line progress." Many late-nineteenth-century
and early-twentieth-century histories (some of them still in
wide use as textbooks) gravely trace an "evolutionary" development from the "simplicities" of primitive and folk
music up a steadily "ascending" path through the "first,
real" art music (by Palestrina or Monteverdi, say) to the
complexity and quasi-"perfection" of symphonies and operas by Beethoven and Wagner.

Put this way, such bogus-evolutionary thinking is self-
evidently nonsensical—*if* the reader has any real knowledge
of primitive and folk musics (which often are exceedingly
complex and always are very different), and of medieval,
Renaissance, and baroque works (beside which even the
most grandiose structures of later composers are, if not
"simple," certainly no more intricate or daring). Nevertheless, the illusion of "progress" is deeply ingrained. It's easy
to forget that art isn't science or technology or industry,
where genuine and steady advances can be made and are indeed sensationally characteristic of the last century or so.
Human nature, emotions, and expressiveness change little
over the years, however—radical as alterations may be in
the means of expression available to or favored by any
given era.

Closely allied to the misleading application of evolution
theory is a distortion of the "survival of the fittest" doctrine.
Whatever standing (if any) this theory retains in biology, it
has none at all in the history of any art, where the determin-

ing factors for survival of any form, medium, or style include abstract "fitness" only in a minor role. To take a familiar example, the piano did *not* "evolve" from the earlier harpsichord (it's a quite different instrument in both operation and sound), and it certainly did not supplant the harpsichord because of any innate superiority. Some two centuries ago musical styles, tastes, and customs changed radically enough for one instrument to usurp public favor while the other lost it almost entirely. But today (and only partially thanks to the powers of electronic amplification), the harpsichord is swiftly returning—not as a substitute for the piano, but as an invaluable complement to it.

I don't dare discuss in detail all the other misleading or erroneous notions likely to becloud our historical outlook, but a few at least should be suggested: that all early art music was exclusively *contrapuntal*, whereas classical, romantic, and contemporary music is exclusively *harmonic;* that the ancients had no instrumental or "popular" (secular) music to speak of; that "program" music dates no farther back than to nineteenth-century romantic composers; and that there is some basic difference, in either kind or quality, between "absolute" or "pure" music and that written to a program or even to words of any kind.

Most of these misconceptions embody some elements of fact, but all of them exaggerate or distort actual facts into dangerous half-truths. Another source of confused thinking (whenever history is sketched in terms of its leading figures) lies in excessive hero worship. We all have a weakness for heroes (and villains, too) in music as elsewhere, but that shouldn't delude us into believing that the "giants" of any age completely "sum up" the work of their predecessors and contemporaries. Usually they did write more great music, but that doesn't mean the others' music was "much the same, only not as good." As Mme Landowska reminds us (and how often that reminder is needed!), "Masterpieces are not wolves and do not devour each other."

Contemporary or later generations evaluate more or less justly according to the tastes of their times, but none of these evaluations (including our own) is absolute or immutable. In any case, the highest rewards of art depend on the enjoyment both of supreme masterpieces and of the characteristic expressions of all kinds of competing personalities— among whom the "minor" artists sometimes are as appealing and illuminating as the "major" figures, and sometimes even more so.

One of the greatest dangers in listening to recorded music is that we're likely to feel that hearing one or two samples of a given period or composer gives us adequate insight into the whole work of the time or man. Happily, the corresponding advantage is that by repeated hearings we soon come to know the "samples" so well that curiosity drives us to extend our scope and to find other, comparable, yet always individual facets of the era or personality in which we're interested.

And it is right here, in close, understanding friendship with the music itself, that the remote names in any kind of history book truly come to life. Establishing their background is immensely valuable, but the background itself is no more than an empty stage until it actually is peopled with the living actors, eloquently voicing their vibrantly dramatic roles in their own personal accents.

ALL analogies in art are dangerous, but, if only as a corrective to the "evolutionary" notions that persist in most of our minds, there is one that may be helpful in thinking of music's changes—and similarities—over the centuries. That is the symbolizing of music as a garden or field tilled by many generations of farmers, which, through the cycling years, lean and rich, has borne many harvests.

Some of these are more memorable than others, but few have been entirely barren. Throughout many decades certain crops have been the main ones. But gradually the soil was worked out, perhaps even abandoned and given over to weeds for a time. Eventually different crops were planted and nourished, and these too flourished for their time, only to give way to still others.

Walking this field today, how dare we assert that the herb, say, it bears now is better, or worse, than the grain of a century ago, or the flax of a century before that, or even the primeval forests and wildflowers that grew here before recorded history began? · ·

It is enough for us to have the bursting storehouse of its harvest over many seasons: some of it to satisfy our most exacting present-day tastes, but all of it nourishing or useful to us—just as it was, whether in the same or in entirely different ways, to our long generations of ancestors.

9. Out of the Shadowed Past

> . . . the deeper we sound, the further down into the lower world of the past we probe and press, the more do we find that the earliest foundations of humanity, its history and culture, reveal themselves unfathomable.
> —MANN: Joseph and His Brothers

A wealth of fascinating literature, old and new, deals with the music of antiquity. Its performers have been vividly described and pictured. We have authentic documents dealing in considerable detail with the theoretical backgrounds and philosophical implications of Greek and Byzantine music in particular. And there can be no doubt whatever that music—instrumental as well as vocal—figured vitally both in the culture of ancient civilizations and in the daily life of all early peoples.

But the most important fact of all is simply and brutally this: we don't know now and probably never will know how any of this music really *sounded*.

Of Greek music, six complete compositions of a hymnlike character (*circa* 138 B.C. to A.D. 130), plus a few fragmentary others, have been preserved, but except to historians these have little practical meaning. Certainly no one who listens today to the recordings of them can catch more than an enigmatic, whispering echo of the far past. How they were sung (and accompanied, if they were accompanied) in their own times remains an impenetrable mystery.

Of the other early civilizations, we have even less—or almost nothing at all from Egypt, Rome, and many others. Only in later Jewish and some Oriental music and the very much later music of the Byzantine and Western branches of the Christian Church is it possible for tonal archaeologists to detect traces of the early elements that went into the centuries-long development of these arts.

The dependence on oral and aural traditions, the lack of adequate notation, and the dominance of the church in the preservation of all learning combine to account for the fact that our only substantial knowledge of the music of the first ten or eleven centuries of the Christian era is concerned with the religious monody or unison song known as *plainsong*. Originally there were several varieties, but we have no authentic phonographic examples of Gallican and Mozarabic chant, and only a few of Ambrosian chant, for which there still is a living tradition today.

Nowadays, apart from the Eastern Christian and Jewish liturgies, plain song is practically synonymous with Gregorian chant—the earliest great music for which a large repertory still exists and which still maintains intact its ancient eloquence. In using the term "ancient," however, we must remember that Gregorian chant is an amalgam of diverse elements fused over many centuries, attaining a golden age in the eleventh to thirteenth centuries, then gradually deteriorating. It is only comparatively recently that the old, pure traditions have been substantially restored, largely through the researches of the Benedictine monks of Solesmes, France, and the official sanction of the 1903 *Motu proprio* of Pope Pius X.

Scholarly debate still rages about many Gregorian details, especially those concerned with rhythm. In actual church practice today there often are lapses from what purists consider strict performance-authenticity, particularly in added organ accompaniments. So while there is a considerable Gregorian disc repertory (still mostly on 78's), much of it cannot be considered genuinely representative.

GOTHIC ORGANUM, ARS ANTIQUA, AND SECULAR MUSIC

The bridge between the strictly monophonic plainsong and *polyphony* (i.e., many voices) was provided by a style called *organum* or *diaphony* (singing together). In this the principal melody (*cantus firmus*, usually drawn from Gregorian chant), was paralleled by another voice part at intervals of a fourth or fifth above or below. This practice probably originated in earlier folk-singing customs, particularly in northern Europe and the British Isles. Possibly it was encouraged by the fact that early medieval organs played in parallel octaves and fifths. It may have appeared in some churches as early as the seventh century, but it did not reach its height until the second half of the twelfth, and then in generally much freer form, approaching the greater independence of voice parts in true polyphony.

At last, in the great school of *ars antiqua* centered in the Cathedral of Notre-Dame in Paris, we reach the first important personalities (apart from theoreticians) who emerge from the incalculable mass of "anonymous and communal" composers of the unknown past: Leo Leoninus, his successor Perotinus, and Franco of Cologne (all late twelfth and possibly early thirteenth century).

It should not be thought, however, that the church had a complete monopoly on music-making, even though we now possess only indirect evidence of what very early popular folk and instrumental music was like. While the music of the Western Church stemmed primarily from Eastern and Near Eastern sources (and for long was exclusively monophonic and modal, and mainly if not exclusively vocal), European secular music was strongly influenced if not dominated by northern (probably Scandinavian and Celtic) traits and materials. This secular music was organized in patterns that later led to what we know today as the major and minor scales, was sung at least sometimes in parts (including the thirds and sixths then forbidden in church music), and generally made use of various instruments in either participating or accompanying part roles.

The principal performers, or at least disseminators, of secular music long were the goliards (wandering clerks and students), minstrels, bards, jongleurs, and jesters who traveled from court to court throughout Europe as professional and semiprofessional entertainers. Later, with the rise of medieval chivalry, came a new kind of musical spokesman: the Provençal *troubadour*, northern French *trouvère*, and (still later) the German *Minnesänger*. Some of these, being royal or noble (Richard the Lion-Hearted is a famous example), often employed professional minstrels to notate and accompany, and perhaps help to compose, their songs. Others, like Bernart de Ventadorn (1130–1195) were of lowly birth, but educated in both poetry and music at one of the knightly courts.

Most of these poet composers' verses and many of their melodies have been preserved, but since the notation of the latter was rudimentary, no one now knows exactly the kind or amount of rhythmic freedom and melodic ornamentation customarily used by the original singers. Nor do we know exactly how they were accompanied, except that various instruments were employed, singly or in combination— among them the minstrel's harp, lute, viol, and vielle.

At any rate, some of these songs have been recorded by modern specialists, but here again many of the best examples are as yet available only on 78's. Yet here, too, despite all the uncertainties about performance styles, at least some of the springlike fervor of this music still comes to life for contemporary listeners.

LATE GOTHIC MUSIC

The thirteenth and fourteenth centuries were a time of almost unparalleled musical ferment as the barriers between religious and secular, vocal and instrumental, began to break down. Singing and dancing dissolved their ancient marriage to go separate ways. The beginnings of music drama (foreshadowed long before in elaborations of the Mass) were made in "mystery" and liturgic plays, and in the entertainments and pastorales that took place outside the confines and control of the church. Popular melodies crept insidiously into the church's own music, while Gregorian melodies were taken over for secular (indeed, often ribald) texts. Polyphonic and other technical devices of "art" (then generally church) composers were increasingly employed in secular music. And all kinds of music aspired to greater rhythmical and melodic freedom, even though many of the new "liberties" (such as chromatic or non-modal tones) were officially forbidden and could not appear overtly in notated religious music.

The most important names here probably are those of Adam de la Halle (c. 1220–87), the last of the trouvères, and—in the fourteenth century—those of the masters of the truly named *ars nova:* Philippe de Vitry (c. 1285–1361), Francesco Landini (c. 1325–97), and particularly Guillaume de Machaut (c. 1300–77). All of these wrote both secular and religious music. Machaut was the first individual ever to compose a complete Mass—a work whose granitic strength still is formidably impressive to our own ears.

No sharp dividing line can be drawn between the medieval and Renaissance eras, which, like all general historical periods, overlapped, and in which the long persistence of many Gothic traditions makes any real musical cleavage meaningless. One other composer should be mentioned, however, as credited for leading strictly Gothic music to "a last impressive culmination." This was the Englishman John Dunstable (c. 1370–1453), now largely associated with the great *Agincourt Hymn.* But that wonderful song may not have been written by him and, in any case, undoubtedly is based on folk materials. Actually, Dunstable was important for religious as well as secular music and wrote many noble works we need to know better today, both for themselves and as indications of the kind of music that in its own day exerted such powerful influence on contemporary composers, Continental as well as British.

And though we are dealing in this section mainly with personalities rather than technical devices, some mention must be given one of the latter which rose toward the end of medievalism to play a vital role in later polyphony. This was the *canon* (in which one voice part follows another in more or less exact imitation), characteristic of a whole out-pouring of immensely popular works known as the *chace* in France, *caccia* in Italy, and *round* in England. These were notable in particular for their rhythmic freedom and ani-mation. Also for the naturalistic character of their texts, which often dealt with hunting, fishing, market and street cries; or the seasons, as in the most famous British example, the "Reading Rota" or round, *Sumer is icumen in*, whose English words and musical spirit unmistakably hail the be-ginnings of a new era—not only in music, but in all art and life itself.

10. With the Tongues of Men and Angels

> *Know, that in my* Younger Time, *we had* Musick *most* excellently choice, *and most* eminently Rare . . . *even such, as* (*if your* Young Tender Ears, *and* Fantacies, *were but truly* Tinctur'd *therewith, and especially if it possibly could but be cry'd up for the* Mode, *or* New Fashion) *you would* Embrace, *for some Divine Thing.*
> —Thomas Mace: *Musicke's Monument* (1676)

And now the loose bands of mostly faceless early music-makers give way to the regiments of established celebrities waiting impatiently in our time-stage's wings. But we should be rash to assume any phenomenal increase in either the quantity (population percentage-wise) or the quality of composers. Not only have most of the names of medieval musicians been lost, but that age deliberately de-emphasized "individualism." Music was made for the glory of God, or for casual fun, and in neither case did an actual composer dream of "creating" something of his "own" or anything worth preserving for future generations.

Many old traditions carried over into the Renaissance, but a distinctive trait of the new age was its then novel stress on individuals as such and on artistic creation as the expression of assertive personalities.

Another trait, perhaps novel only to us, was the internationalism of all art. Most of the music we know today is that of Western civilization only, developed in or near Europe, but the various communities of Renaissance Europe were parochial rather than strongly nationalistic. Nearly all leading composers traveled widely and were versed not only in the "universal" language, Latin, but in several of the increasingly important popular tongues. So, while it is convenient to speak of the Burgundian and Flemish schools dominating early Renaissance music, we must remember that their main activities were centered in Italy, some of the men themselves were of neither Burgundian nor Flemish birth, and in any case many of them lived at various times all over Europe and the British Isles.

Apart from Dunstable (and some others associated with the Henry V group in England), Gilles Binchois (*c.* 1400–60) and Guillaume Dufay (*c.* 1400–74) are the first great names here. Binchois was one of the first "celebrities" (except for the troubadours) to write comparatively little religious music, favoring the popular secular forms of late medievalism: *chanson, ballade, rondeau,* and so on. Dufay, however, wrote prolifically both in these forms and in those of the religious *motet* and *Mass.* Many of his Masses bear such entrancing names as *Se la face ay pale, Douce Mémoire,* and *L'Homme armé,* drawn from the secular tunes that he used (in accordance with a then common practice) as *canti firmi.*

Dufay's pupil, Jan Ockeghem (*c.* 1430–95) led the first Flemish school, but he and his colleagues Jacob Obrecht (*c.* 1430–1505) and Heinrich Finck (1455-1527) exemplified many startling stylistic changes. Instead of only three voice parts in their polyphonic works, these men generally used

four and occasionally many more—thirty-six in one of Ockeghem's giant canons! Indeed, their contrapuntal techniques became so elaborate and intricate that their music
still has a notorious reputation for "scholarly" complexity.
It is probably on this count that so little of it is performed
or recorded today. But before condemning them unheard,
we might well remember that Bach himself long was considered far too "dry and intellectual" for the general listener.

When the line of Flemish succession passed to Ockeghem's
pupil Josquin des Prés (c. 1445–1521), stylistic ideals shifted
again, this time back to a more "classical" clarity and sym-
metry, a more precise and equable control of complex materials, and an abandonment of the old, easygoing custom
of mixing instruments and voices more or less indiscrimi-
nately.

Best-remembered today for his church music, Josquin
happily is also represented on LP's by some of his secular
chansons, which give us a more rounded appreciation of
this "Prince of Music's" full stature. But we are usually able
to hear his great contemporary Hendrik Isaac (c. 1450–
1517) only in a few of his lovely German songs, though he
also wrote in many other styles and languages.

Josquin's pupil Nicolas Gombert (c. 1500–c.1555), and
the Flemish founder of later Viennese and Venetian schools,
Adrien Willaert (c. 1480–1562), turned away from the serenity of Josquin to write with a passion and dramatic force
that foreshadowed the baroque age, particularly in anticipations of an *antiphonal* style, in which choruses were split
up into sections that sang sometimes alternately, sometimes
together. And Willaert also was a pioneer in the development of the "vocal chamber music" form, the *madrigal*,
which was to flower so richly by the end of this fabulous
sixteenth century.

RENAISSANCE TO BAROQUE

The last third of the century was dominated by two giants
(as Bach and Handel were to co-rule a later age): the last
of the great Flemish masters, Orlandus Lassus (c. 1530–94),

and the first of the Romans, Giovanni da Palestrina (*c.* 1524–94).

Lassus, like Handel a man of the world, was proficient and prolific in all forms and languages, the outstanding musical figure of his time, honored all over Europe as no musician had been before (and few have since). And though few present-day listeners yet know any of his some two thousand works (or perhaps even his name!), the steadily growing phonographic repertory of his incalculably varied music holds the promise that his fame may yet flame anew.

Palestrina, of course, is better remembered—though more often by the dubious sobriquet of the "first modern" composer than by a rounded representation of his living music. Like Bach, Palestrina led a remarkably quiet, even prosaic life, but his accomplishments were both enormous and versatile. And as with Mozart, the very perfection of his workmanship and the surface serenity of much of his work have tended, in their luminous beauty, to obscure the true grandeur of his expressive power.

Tracing the mainstream of this golden age, we necessarily ignore a host of other personalities who hardly can be considered minor, as in any other time almost any one of them might have been dominant in his own right. The following summary can do no more than hint at the variety and richness of their genius.

Among the Flemings only Clemens non Papa (*c.* 1510–57) —that is, not Pope Clement—is occasionally represented on discs nowadays. But the masters of the French madrigal or polyphonic chanson fare somewhat better: Clément Jannequin (*c.* 1485–1560), Claude de Sermisy (*c.* 1490–1562), Jacques Arcadelt (*c.* 1514–*c.* 1570), Claude le Jeune (*c.* 1528–1600), and Guillaume Costeley (1531–1606), among many others besides Lassus himself, and the less-well-represented French Huguenot psalm-composer Claude Goudimel (*c.* 1505–72).

The Reformation brought a flood of music in the chorale form that was to play so germinal a part in the works of Bach and other German baroque composers. Martin Luther

(1483–1546) himself often is credited with some of the most famous melodies, but the more important strictly musical names probably are those of his adviser, Johann Walther (1496–1570), and Hans Leo Hassler (1564–1612). The latter also was notable, with the earlier Finck and Isaac, in the development of the German madrigal, or polyphonic *Lied*, as were Johannes Eccard (1553–1611) and Ludwig Senfl (*c.* 1492–*c.* 1555). The last-named, a Swiss German, also wrote for Catholic Church services, as did—exclusively— Jacobus Gallus, sometimes known as Handl (1550–91).

After Palestrina, the big names of Roman church music were those of Giovanni Maria Nanino (*c.* 1545–1607), Marc' Antonio Ingegneri (*c.* 1545–92), and Felice Anerio (*c.* 1560– 1614). The longer list of secular—particularly madrigal— composers was led (after Lassus and Palestrina) by Orazio Vecchi (*c.* 1550–1605), Luca Marenzio (*c.* 1560–99), and the fabulous murderer prince Carlo Gesualdo (*c.* 1560– 1614). Monteverdi, who also belongs here, will be saved for the next chapter, and Willaert has been mentioned earlier; but the latter shared fame with the German-born Gregor Aichinger (1565–1628), and the Gabrielis, uncle and neph- ew, Andrea (*c.* 1510–86) and Giovanni (1557–1613), who brought polychoral techniques to their height, not only in vocal choruses, but also in massive display works for brass ensembles.

Among the Spaniards, Tomás Luis de Victoria (*c.* 1535– 1611), obscured by the fame of his contemporary, Pales- trina, often suffers the further indignity of losing his true name for the Italianized form, Vittoria. But to hear his music itself (exclusively in Mass or motet form) is to dis- cover unparalleled depths of dramatic passion which exert a very special appeal on modern ears. And his timeliness of expressive power well may be shared by his nearly equally great compatriot Cristóbal Morales (1500–53), once the latter's work is made more accessible on records.

The English school begun by Dunstable grew to include the mighty names of, first, Thomas Tallis (*c.* 1505–85), too often remembered today only by Vaughan Williams's use of one of his themes; then, William Byrd (1542-1623), whose eloquent church music for both Roman and Anglican rites only recently has been representatively recorded. Other British church musicians like John Taverner (*c.* 1495–1545) and Christopher Tye (*c.* 1500–*c.* 1572) still have to be revived, at least on records. John Merbecke (*c.* 1523–85) was perhaps less important musically than historically for his contributions to Anglican chant.

The most famous British works, however, were secular: the ayres of the lutenists, of whom the Irish-born John Dowland (1563–1626) was the most notable, and the madrigals of an incredibly gifted group of Elizabethans. Thomas Morley (1557–*c.* 1603) and Orlando Gibbons (1583–1625) —along with Byrd—probably are the best-known of these today, but even they cannot eclipse the extraordinary genius of Thomas Tomkins (1573–1656), John Wilbye (1574–1638), and—perhaps most remarkable of them all—Thomas Weelkes (*c.* 1575–1623).

SIXTEENTH-CENTURY INSTRUMENTAL MUSIC

Besides the upheaval of its Himalayan peaks of vocal polyphony, this age also marks the rise of perhaps the first significant foothills of the great range of purely instrumental music of our own day. Instruments had been widely used (contrary to a popular misconception) from the very beginnings of music history, and many of them had been highly developed by, if not before, the sixteenth century. But it was then that they seemed suddenly to call forth many works of distinctive originality, which also revealed clearly autonomous — rather than vocally dependent — stylistic techniques.

There were even approaches to the orchestra, not only in the Gabrielis' brass ensembles, but in larger, more heterogeneous aggregations including recorders, oboes, bassoons, and horns, with or without a variety of stringed instruments. But much of this experimentation was in performance only, where the only current curbs were those of practicality (for "scoring" then was largely a matter of players' choice). Except for some music for viol ensembles (or "consorts," as they were called in England), most works intended for specific performance media were written for solo instruments.

One of the most popular of these solo instruments was the lute (or, in Spain, the *vihuela*), for which the outstanding specialists (lutenists or *vihuelistas*) were—besides Dowland— Jean-Baptiste Besard (*c.* 1565–*c.* 1625) and Luis Milan (*c.* 1500–65). But there were many others, such as the Frenchman Pierre Attaignant (fl. 1525–49)—who, however, may only have edited or collected most of the pieces published over his name—and the Spaniard Alonso de Mudarra (fl. 1546), who also wrote for the solo harp.

As the old vielles died out, the singularly sweet- if weaktoned elder brothers of the violins and cellos known to us reigned briefly until public taste shifted to the greater brilliance and sonority of the latter. The viols, especially the *viola da gamba*, lived on for some time, however. Bach and Handel wrote for them, as they also did for another favorite of this era, the *recorder* (an early, "straight" flute). And in our own day there has been a great revival of interest in both these instrumental families. Long considered obsolete, apparently they have been only hibernating, awaiting another change in the "climate" of listeners' tastes.

Developments of the long-popular organ foreshadowed the even greater strides to be made in the following century. Many notable works were written, especially in *variation*, *toccata*, and *ricercare* forms, by the Venetian Gabrielis, the Spaniard Antonio Cabezón (1510–66), the Englishman John Bull (*c.* 1562–1628), the Italian Claudio Merulo (1533– 1604), the Austrian Paul Hofhaimer (1459–1537), and— perhaps greatest of them all—the Dutchman Sweelinck and the Italian Frescobaldi, who will be discussed later.

Of the other two great keyboard instruments, the clavichord, although by far the older, was largely passed over by composers of this period, except perhaps for improvisation and practice. But, like the organ (with which much of its music was at first interchangeable), the harpsichord developed a true keyboard technique as distinct from the quasi-vocal polyphony that previously had furnished most of its material. Here, again, England was outstanding during this period, with a wealth of fascinating literature for the *virginal*, or virginals, as this little table-top harpsichord usually was somewhat mysteriously called. The major contributors were John Bull, the organist; Morley, Gibbons, Tomkins, and especially Byrd, of the madrigalists; and Giles Farnaby (*c.* 1560–*c.* 1600). Some of their works are chiefly remarkable as the beginnings of keyboard virtuosity, others as naïve but often irresistibly charming examples of programmatic or depictive writing, and many for their toe tickling dance and march rhythms.

There is a special interest in sixteenth-century instrumental music for all kinds of present-day listeners, who can hear in it many startling anticipations of the later repertories they know and love so well. Yet while it certainly warrants attention on this score, as well as for its own distinctive attractions, it never should be allowed to distract our first concern with the same period's infinitely greater achievements in unaccompanied vocal music. Far from "anticipating" anything later, the vocal works represent the final perfection of a whole tone-art. Their sublimity is not only the glory of this luxuriantly creative age, but a wholly unique monument to the expressive powers of the human mind.

11. The Magnificent Experimenters

A moving arabesque that has a vital dimension, an audible mathematics, adding sense to form, and a versification that, since it has no subject-matter, cannot do violence to it by its complex artifices—these are types of pure living, altogether joyful and delightful things.
—SANTAYANA: *Reason in Art*

IT was only for clarity of our bird's-eye view that I extended the discussion of Renaissance music into the seventeenth century. The start of the age now generally called *baroque* probably dates from around 1560. Even Lassus and Palestrina sometimes are included in the later rather than the earlier period, while Monteverdi and Sweelinck seem to stand astride both. But one thing is sure: while 1600 is a convenient turning-point in music history, it scarcely deserves its present popular fame as the dividing marker between "ancient" and "modern" music.

In any case, the turn did not hinge exclusively on the so-called "birth" of opera in the activities of the Florentine school of *nuove musiche*. Actually, the much-publicized "new" works, like those of many other musical "revolutions" and "reforms," were largely reactionary in nature. At best they were straws blown before the rising winds of new tastes and style. The Florentines were mostly literary men and dilettantes like Jacopo Peri (1561–1633) and Jacopo Corsi (*c.* 1560–*c.* 1604). Their group (*camerata*) did include one professional, Giulio Caccini (1548–1618), but he was a decidedly minor composer.

The baroque era became, certainly, the first great age of opera (and oratorio and cantata), but, just as importantly, it also was the first great age of "independent" instrumental music. It was notable above all for a final shift in the balance of power between church music and that composed in secular "art" (as distinct from folk and popular) forms. Yet the latter's predilection for harmonic rather than contrapuntal techniques did not immediately overthrow the polyphonic traditions (which were to reach new, if different, heights in Bach and Handel). And the "new" styles themselves clearly were the outgrowth of a concern with the possibilities of verbal and melodic expressiveness and other "representational" trends, which had fascinated many much earlier composers.

The baroque in music, then, is characterized less by any revolutionary developments than by its strong but gradual shifts in stylistic emphasis, and particularly by the boldness and freedom with which its minor as well as major spokesmen experimented with both old and new resources.

The specialized trend vociferously proclaimed by the Florentine *camerata* can be traced and appreciated much better in the works of greater musicians, especially Claudio Monteverdi (1567–1643). For while his motets and madrigals were deeply rooted in the older traditions, his operas clearly were in the newer fashion—although of course they too carried over many earlier techniques, freely adapted to meet changing conditions and purposes.

Many other Italians rose to importance around this time, quite possibly because the new trends were more congenial to the Italian temperament than those of the Renaissance— which had been largely expressed by composers of northern origins, even if of Italian training. But though these "new" Italians are most often remembered today by their dramatic works, most of them also wrote in the strictly polyphonic, older church styles.

Two outstanding masters were Giacomo Carissimi (1605– 74), leader of the Roman school, best known for his cantatas and oratorios, and the Neapolitan Alessandro Scarlatti (1659–1725), who wrote prolifically and fluently in all forms, instrumental as well as vocal. Other notable figures included Steffano Landi (c. 1590–c. 1655), Domenico Mazzocchi (1592–1665), Marc' Antonio Cesti (1618–69), Giovanni Legrenzi (1626–90), Alessandro Stradella (c. 1645– 1682), and Giovanni Bassani (1657–1716).

In strictly instrumental music, the outstanding Italians of the early baroque were (besides A. Scarlatti) the organist Girolamo Frescobaldi (1583–1643), the violinist Arcangelo Corelli (1653–1713)—whose solo and ensemble works for strings still are frequently performed—and the organist and harpsichordist Bernardo Pasquini (1637–1710).

In England there was a mixture of strong Italian influences (especially in writing for strings) and characteristically native elements in the music of the Lawes brothers, William (1582–1645) and Henry (1595–1662), Matthew Locke (*c.* 1632–77), John Blow (1649–1708), and Blow's pupil Henry Purcell (*c.* 1659–1695)—the first truly outstanding figure in British music after the sudden extinction of the Elizabethan school, and indeed almost the only one until many years later.

Few real operas were written in England (apart from Purcell's superb *Dido and Æneas*). The popular dramatic form, especially during the Restoration, was the *masque*—an entertainment, probably of Italian origin, which combined music with miming and dancing in sometimes highly spectacular fashion. A degenerated variety of the madrigal, often with bawdy texts, called the *catch*, also was popular. Blow wrote much church music, as well as masques, but Purcell was the only Englishman of this time who wrote vital music in a wide variety of forms—among them the string *fantasias* beloved by the Elizabethans, which in their purely polyphonic style are much more characteristic of the Renaissance than of the baroque age itself.

In France the Italian influence was even stronger. Indeed, the outstanding early baroque composer was the Italian-born Jean-Baptiste Lully (1632–87). He wrote many operas and ballets, but his fame now rests largely on their instrumental passages, especially on the so-called *French overture*. This became an enormously popular form among baroque composers, and it is highly significant for us, not only for the superb musical examples still played and recorded today, but also as one of the basic cornerstones of the whole "modern" symphonic style.

Few strictly instrumental composers of note are well remembered from this period in France, apart from Jacques Champion de Chambonnières (1602–72), pioneer if not father of the later rococo school of harpsichordists. But recently the phonograph has resurrected appealing works by two men lost even from most history books: the Rouen organist Jean Titelouze (1563–1633) and the "King's lutenist" Robert de Visée (*c*. 1650–*c*. 1725).

There were fewer Italian influences in northern than in southern German and Austrian music, and even these probably stemmed less from Rome than from the Venetian school of the earlier Willaert and the Gabrielis. The first outstanding name is that of the Dutch organist and church-music composer Jan Pieterzoon Sweelinck (1562–1621), who may have studied in Venice, but obviously also was well versed in British virginalists' techniques, as still may be noted in his magnificent variations and fantasias. He is perhaps best considered historically, however, as a link between the old and the new eras. It is the next master, Heinrich Schütz (1585–1672), who must be credited with initiating a distinctively German baroque style, and of towering (with the later Buxtehude) not only among the predecessors of Bach, but among the supreme giants of all time.

Schütz wrote in many forms, but he remains best known for his sacred passions, motets, and cantatas—many of which are available in recorded performances that give modern listeners at least some notion of the profound expressive depths in his music. Yet in his day two contemporaries were esteemed nearly as highly: Johann Hermann Schein (1586–1630) and Samuel Scheidt (1587–1654)—the other two of the popularly grouped three great "S's" that antedated our own far more incongruously allied three "B's."

Mention also should be made of Michael Praetorius (1571–1621), the south Germans Andreas Hammerschmidt (1612–75) and Johann Jacob Frohberger (*c*. 1617–67), the Alsatian Jan Reincken (1623–1722)—a special favorite of Bach's — another notable organist, Matthias Weckmann

(1621–74), and the "*Stadtpfeiffer*" Johann Pezel (1639–94), in whose sturdy pieces for brass ensembles we can catch a thrilling echo of the municipal ceremonial music so relished in those days and so ideally suited to out-of-door performance.

But it was a Dane, Dietrich Buxtehude (1637–1707), who perhaps best represented the northern high-baroque style. Happily, much of his music has lately been rescued from the reputation it long has had of merely pre-Bach historical interest. Hearing his boldly dramatic solo and choral cantatas and his vaulting organ works today, we can re-establish his distinctive personality as that of an unparalleled master of the grand style.

LATER BAROQUE ERA

Moving into the second half of this period, and before we return to the energetic continuing activities in Italy, I should mention such notables as Johann Pachelbel (1653–1706), especially for his organ works in the chorale-prelude form now so closely associated with Bach; Vincent Lübeck (1654–1740), Johann Philipp Krieger (1649–1725), and the more obscure Johann Christoph Kriedel (fl. 1700), all of whom can be reheard to some extent, mainly in cantatas, today; Johann Kuhnau (1660–1722), famed for his "anticipations" of many devices of later "program"-music; Georg Böhm (1661–1733) and Johann Gottfried Walther (1684–1748), who wrote mostly keyboard works; Reinhard Keiser (1674–1739), the first important name in German opera; Heinrich von Biber (1644–1704), Johann Ernst Galliard (*c.* 1687–1749), and Johann Rosenmüller (1620–84), who, especially Rosenmüller, made vital contributions to instrumental sonata and suite repertories; and the fabulous Georg Philipp Telemann (1681–1767), quite possibly the most prolific composer who ever lived.

In Italy Alessandro Scarlatti was followed by (besides his son, Domenico, to be discussed later) a flood of composers who wrote both church and secular works in both vocal and instrumental forms: Antonio Lotti (1667–1740), Tomasso Albinoni (1674–1745), Giovanni Battista Bononcini (1672–*c*. 1750), Francesco Durante (1684–1755), the Marcellos—Alessandro (1684–1750) and Benedetto (1686–1739)—Niccolò Porpora (1686–1767), Leonardo Leo (1694–1744), and many others. But the Italian music of this period which seems to have demonstrated the strongest survival powers is that for instruments only, the violin in particular. Besides some of those composers named above, other notable names are those of Francesco Geminiani (1667–1762), Giuseppe Valentini (1681-*c*. 1740), Giuseppe Tartini (1692–1770), and Pietro Locatelli (1693–1764).

None of these can be said to rank among the great masters, as does the last of the Italian baroque composers, Antonio Vivaldi (*c*. 1675–1741). Yet it has been only in recent years that performances (particularly on records) have begun to represent the immense range of dramatic imagination revealed in his vocal works as well as those in concerto, *concerto grosso*, and sonata forms.

Apart from England's adopted son Handel, the only important late-baroque British figure was Dr. William Boyce (1710–79). He was long considered a minor composer of church music, but it was quite recently discovered that he wrote a group of "symphonies" whose breadth and brilliance remind modern listeners of both Purcell and Bach, yet with an unmistakable individual accent all their own.

A somewhat comparable Frenchman was Michel Richard de Lalande (1657–1726), whose magnificent *De Profundis* shakes our faith in the æsthetic qualifications of historians who have relegated him to something considerably less than a top rank outside French music itself. André Campra (1660–1744) was perhaps the most important French opera-composer between Lully and Rameau. Most of the others, like Jean-Baptiste Lœillet (1680–1730), the Flemish-born flute composer, were of relatively minor importance until we reach Rameau and Couperin—who can be more conveniently considered in the next chapter.

Any chapter on the baroque era inevitably must close with the paired giants who were both apotheosis and completion of the age, who—fairly or unfairly—generally are singled out to represent the entire period. It is highly misleading to think of Johann Sebastian Bach (1685–1750) and George Frideric Handel (1685–1759) as summing up all their predecessors' music, or completely overshadowing the oftentimes unique personalities of their elders and contemporaries. Yet it certainly is true that between these two Titans almost every form explored by others was mined practically to exhaustion.

It would be futile to try to sound here any new pæans to their greatness. It must be enough to repeat once more that the music of each represents a pole or hemisphere of the world of their time. Neither was an innovator in any strict sense of the word, but everything they touched was transformed by their incomparable genius.

From Bach we have all the forms beloved of the north European baroque—cantatas, Passions, Masses, motets, organ chorale-preludes, display toccatas and fugues; distinctive translations and augmentations of French and Italian styles in chamber and solo instrumental works, and larger-scaled orchestral suites and concertos; and, in addition to all these, those tremendous explorations of the ultimate resources of polyphonic writing (and of the organizing power of the human mind): *The Well-Tempered Clavier*, *A Musical Offering*, and *The Art of Fugue*.

From Handel we have a still scarcely appraised wealth of chamber music for both small and large (sometimes even grandiose) ensembles, as well as scores of operas and oratorios, some in German and many in Italian styles, but the last and most magnificent in a distinctively new blend of these with characteristically English elements—of which the enormous popularity of *Messiah* and a few others unfortunately has blinded most modern listeners to other treasures as yet enjoyed by comparatively few Handel specialists.

' But here—unlike the situation where so many other outstanding names of this and earlier eras are concerned —much of Handel's and perhaps most of Bach's music are increasingly generously represented on LP recordings. And these works speak for themselves and for their composers far more persuasively and eloquently than any commentator ever can hope to do.

12. Gallantry, Enlightenment, Revolt

From the depth of sentiment comes the clarity of form and from the strength of the mood comes the spirituality of its atmosphere. This harmony of spirit springs forth from the soul and finds expression or blossoms forth in the form of music.

—The Wisdom of Confucius

IF THE gigantic monuments erected by Bach and Handel were the glories of the baroque era, they also were its tombstones. Even during his lifetime Bach came to be considered old-fashioned, and his music soon was obscured by that of his sons, who turned the training he had given them to new purposes and ideals. Handel fared better, largely because he had sensed the reaction against the artificiality of Italian-style opera and had developed a more straightforwardly dramatic form of oratorio. But it was mainly outside England that composers veered most sensitively before the shifts in the winds of musical tastes. They realized that a new mass listening public demanded less serious and complex entertainment, that it was becoming increasingly responsive to direct expressions of peronalized individual feeling.

To meet the new demand they developed a *style galant,* which ran like a bright ribbon not only through the so-called *rococo* music of the early and middle eighteenth century, but also in that of many later composers, including Mozart and even some twentieth-century Frenchmen. And to exploit the new sensibility they began to experiment with what was called a *style bourgeois*, which soon led, first to a period of somewhat misleadingly named "classical" music, and later—but without any real break—into the more aptly named "romantic" era.

The most notable features of this eighteenth-century blend of rococo, classical, and romantic elements probably were: a turning away from contrapuntal writing and polyphonic forms; a marked increase in composing for solo instruments and specific types of small ensembles; a growing tendency to score performers' parts in full detail (rather than depending on traditional interpretation codes like "ornament" signs and "figured basses"); the formation of the symphony orchestra (without supporting harpsichord) much as we know it today; and an intensified concern with wider, more subtle ranges of both tonal coloring and dynamic contrasts.

The rococo spirit was revealed to perfection in the little harpsichord "sonatas" by Domenico Scarlatti (1685–1757), one of the first to compose almost exclusively for a single instrument. He directly inspired a group of Spanish followers, but few of these are well known today, except perhaps Antonio Soler (1739–83), for the younger Scarlatti's music was so highly individualized, so perfect in itself and so "modern" in spirit that its full influence wasn't felt until much later times.

Of more immediate significance was a group of Frenchmen, who exhibited a wider range of characteristic, if less distinctive, rococo qualities. One of the most important was François Couperin (1668–1733), whose popular nickname, "*le grand*," seems inept nowadays unless we know his great, unmistakably baroque choral works or the chamber concertos which blend many aspects of both the earlier and the newer ages. For we are most accustomed to hearing his harpsichord miniatures, famous for their bubbling vivacity and poetically depictive titles.

The other great name was that of Jean-Philippe Rameau
(1683–1764), who also stood astride the two periods: baroque in many of his operas, rococo in his harpsichord
pieces, and something of both in his ensemble works. But
even the best of his music, at least for many years, probably
had less influence on his contemporaries and successors
than his writings on music theory.

Of lesser fame, for all the delightfulness of much of
their music, were Jean-François Dandrieu (1681–1738),
Louis-Claude Daquin (1694–1772), and Jean-Marie Leclair
(1697–1764), all of whom wrote mostly instrumental music;
the opera- and ballet-composers Pierre-Alexandre Monsigny (1729–1817), François Gossec (1734–1829), André
Grétry (1741–1813), and that famous advocate of a "return
to nature" Jean-Jacques Rousseau (1712–78), who is best
remembered today for his literary *Confessions*.

The sensational popularity of these last men's light or
"comic" stage works exemplified, if it did not actually
lead to, the success of similar works elsewhere. But the
similarity was in spirit: the "local coloring" and accent
varied widely, for—like most music aimed directly at a
large, urban public—such entertainments assumed distinctive national characteristics much more readily than serious
"art" music. In England, for example, "ballad-opera" became all the rage, paced by the undying *Beggar's Opera*, for
which John Gay was the librettist and John Christopher
Pepusch (1667–1752) the composer—or, more accurately,
the editor and arranger of its mostly folk and popular song
materials. There were many others, but few of them are
remembered today, except for some of the less lusty and
more masquelike works of Dr. Thomas Arne (1710–78).
Their influence, however, and particularly that of *The
Beggar's Opera* itself, was reflected back on the French school
of *opéra comique* composers and those of German *Singspiele*—
in which the only name of consequence (until we reach
Mozart) was that of Johann Adam Hiller (1728–1804).

In Italy, where comic opera had originated from the
intermezzi of serious operas, the form was known as *opera*

buffa. One of the earliest examples was the witty, still performed *Serva padrona* by Giovanni Battista Pergolesi (1710–36). Pergolesi, like Couperin and Rameau, harks back to the baroque era in his church music and seems to span the old and new ages in his chamber and orchestral works. Also esteemed in their own times for their light operas, although more often heard today in instrumental works, were Baldassare Galuppi (1706–85), Giovanni Paisiello (1740–1816), and Domenico Cimarosa (1749–1801).

The great composers of serious Italian—or then international—opera have paid dearly for their lifetime fame, for they now are remembered (if at all) mainly as the predecessors, rivals, and followers of Gluck. Even the phonograph has given us little chance to estimate for ourselves such men as Pietro Domenico Paradisi (1710–92), whom we know only by a few harpsichord pieces; the "Italian Gluck," Niccolò Jommelli (1714–74); Nicola Piccini (1728–1800), Gluck's great rival in Paris; Giuseppe Sarti (1729–1802), Antonio Sacchini (1734–86), and Antonio Salieri (1750–1875).

Gluck's own master, Giovanni Battista Sammartini (1701–75), fares but little better, at least as far as his operatic and church works are concerned. He is better represented in instrumental music, as is the other outstanding instrumental composer of the time, Luigi Boccherini (1743–1805), and even such lesser men as Pietro Nardini (1722–93), Gaetano Pugnani (1731–98), and Jean Baptiste Viotti (1753–1824), the last three kept alive mainly in violin virtuosos' recitals.

The fame of every eighteenth-century name mentioned so far is shaded by the master who most closely linked Italian and French musical activities with those (to be discussed in a moment) in Germany and Austria: the German-born, Italian-trained operatic monarch of both Paris and Vienna, Christoph Willibald Gluck (1714–87). He contributed immeasurably—in his overtures and orchestral accompaniments—both to the rapidly developing art of instrumentation and to the formulation of atmospheric, emotionally expressive techniques essential to the music of later, often mainly symphonic composers. And while his last great operas may not invariably have exemplified in practice the "reform" theories for which Gluck is celebrated, they surely did represent many of the basic ideals of a truly "classical" tone-art.

BACH'S SONS AND THE MANNHEIMERS

Before we are ready for the more familiar, if perhaps less justly labeled classical giants, Haydn and Mozart, we should turn back to review earlier German and Austrian activities, particularly those of Bach's sons and the Mannheimers.

The former did not constitute a "school": despite their common background and training, the sons went separate ways and developed individual musical personalities. Of these, the most striking was that of the eldest, Wilhelm Friedemann Bach (1710–84). But he never fulfilled his great promise, and remains—with his less gifted half-brother Johann Christoph Friedrich (1732–93)—a minor figure, at least in contrast with the third and youngest sons, Carl Philipp Emanuel (1714–88) and Johann Christian (1735–82).

The latter (called the "Milan" or "London" Bach) was important historically not only for his works in many forms, but for his influence on Mozart and as the first man to give (at London in 1768) a public concert of the kind that soon was to attain such immense popularity, the piano recital.

C. P. E. Bach, who completely overshadowed his father in the eighteenth century, still must be ranked, if not that high, as one of the most original and influential (as well as famous) composers of his age. He, too, wrote in many forms, but his favorite vehicle was the ancient, wonderfully sensitive and expressive, if delicate-toned *clavichord*, soon to be superseded—even more completely than the harpsichord—by the piano. He is not badly represented on records by chamber and orchestral works (and the dramatic, post-baroque *Magnificat*), but we still lack adequate LP versions of his clavichord pieces—more valuable to our ears for their surprisingly romantic tone-poetry than for their historically more celebrated contributions to "sonata form."

The Mannheimers were more truly a "school" and a powerfully influential one in the development of strictly symphonic music, though for many years they were obscured by the fame of Haydn and Mozart. Despite its members' diverse backgrounds, this group clearly inaugurated the great tradition, generally known as Viennese, which was to dominate orchestral music for a century or more. The outstanding composers of this school probably were: Johann Stamitz (1717–57), Franz Xaver Richter (1709–89), Anton Filtz (c. 1730–60), Christian Cannabich (1731–98), and Stamitz's sons, Karl (1746–1801) and Anton (1754–c. 1809). With these (and Sammartini and Boccherini), Christian Wagenseil (1715–77) must be credited with the highest development of the sonata-symphony form prior to Haydn.

HAYDN, MOZART, BEETHOVEN, SCHUBERT, AND OTHERS

There is no need to linger over the incomparable achievements of Franz Joseph Haydn (1732–1809) and Wolfgang Amadeus Mozart (1756–91), who are much too well known to require further gloss here. Each was a true child of his age, each was a true giant in the sense of excelling in an immense variety of musical forms and media, and each is richly represented in the phonographic repertory.

Yet is is only recently that present-day listeners have begun to get a comprehensive view of their full range. Haydn, in particular, too often has been known by a handful of symphonies, quartets, and oratorios only—until (paced by the Haydn Society) recordings at last began to reveal almost all facets of his multitudinous genius. And with Mozart we are now coming to know not only the master of the last symphonies, quartets, and operas, but the equally inspired and perhaps even more endearingly galant, dramatic magician of the piano concertos, the earlier symphonies, and a whole treasure-house of divertimentos, serenades and other smaller works, all of which gush from an unfailing wellspring of eternal youthfulness, imagination, and passion.

The supreme risk in surveying the richly creative last half of this century is less that of not paying adequate tribute to its unanimously accepted masters than that of overlooking or minimizing their contemporaries and predecessors. These "minor" figures have been relegated to a line or two in reference books, yet—given the opportunity—we often can hear in their music the lively accents of far more than merely "historical" personalities. Unfortunately, however, I too can only mention in passing such remarkable men—of such diverse origins, accomplishments, and characteristics—as Haydn's brother Michael (1737–1806), Karl Ditters von Dittersdorf (1739–99), Johann Abram Schulz (1747–1800), Muzio Clementi (1752–1832), Jan Dussek (1761–1812), and Johann Hummel (1778–1837). Also the opera-composers Étienne Méhul (1763–1817) and Gasparo Spontini (1774–1851), and that much maligned but often startlingly impressive "academician" Luigi Cherubini (1760–1842).

It is Ludwig van Beethoven (1770–1827), of course, who generally is considered to sum up the whole age so loosely called "classical." Indeed, he did crown it with its greatest glory—at the very time he was implacably exhausting and discarding it. Although he was in the direct line of quasi-royal succession in the Viennese musical tradition, I often feel that he can be best understood as primarily a revolutionist spokesman for the dawning age of democratic individualism. He was the first major arch-romanticist, certainly, strongly as he clung to the classical ideals of strict logic and a "universally" intelligible eloquence.

And if another seemingly paradoxical point of view doesn't disturb you, you also may find it illuminating to think of Franz Schubert (1797–1828) less as the romanticist of the songs for which he was so long mainly esteemed than (in his instrumental works at least) as the last of the classical masters. Far less influential than the incredibly forceful Beethoven, this serene and humble melodist may well have built—particularly in his great C major Symphony—the final monument of this age. Surely his lucidity and breadth and sweetness best reconcile the *style galant* and the *style bourgeois.* His finest music voices the fundamental spirit of the eighteenth century—the age of, above all, *enlightenment,* and a profound love both of nature and of all humanity.

13. *Our Fabulous Grandfathers*

> *The lack of expression is perhaps the greatest enormity of all. I should prefer music to say something other than it should, rather than it should say nothing at all.*
> —Rousseau: *Dictionary of Music*

APPROACHING our own times, we reach the music of the "near" past—the music we know best of all, if sometimes at second rather than first hand, and which has largely colored and shaped all of our musical experience. Because it is so close, it is almost impossibly difficult to see in clear perspective. Let us try, however, to maintain our larger point of view for at least a moment longer and to glimpse, if we can, some of the over-all patterns in which its chaotic details might be integrated.

Certainly the nineteenth century as a whole is characterized by the accelerating growth of ultraromanticism, an uncurbed frankness of self-expression, and increased reliance on flamboyant coloring; by the stepped-up development of instruments, of executant techniques, and of virtuoso performers (including for the first time as a star the orchestral conductor); and by the establishment, as a habitual custom, of the practice of presenting non-ritual music in large concert halls and opera houses to immense audiences of heterogeneous listeners.

Viewed more objectively in the future, it may be that this will be considered an "interim" age when the mainstream of music was diverted from its natural course, to be restored to more normal channels only after many years of labor—of which our own are perhaps the beginning. But even those of us who cherish so unorthodox a theory hardly are able to muster convincing proof. Anyway, the significant, unassailable fact is that the vast bulk of the music we hear today (whether we consider it an offshoot or the finest flowering of the great musical tradition) was written either by nineteenth-century composers or those of a younger generation dominated—positively or negatively—by their imperious fathers and grandfathers.

The outstanding musical ultraromanticists were Carl Maria von Weber (1786–1826), Hector Berlioz (1803–69), Frédéric Chopin (1810–49), Robert Schumann (1810–56), Franz Liszt (1811–86), and Richard Wagner (1813–83).

To any widely experienced listener, the music of these men now has become so familiar—if not indeed "old-fashioned"—that he finds it hard to remember the electrifying force of its first impact on him, and even harder to imagine its sensational effect on its astounded, enraptured, and enraged first audiences. The price for its dramatic triumphs is still being paid in the public's reaction against its great former idols and bogeymen.

Yet no one can deny the phenomenal power of these men. They not only made history; they significantly reshaped the minds of listeners for many years. Even today, at perhaps their lowest ebb, Chopin and Schumann still are the staple diet on which every pianist is raised, and their prodigal contributions (particularly the former's harmonic and the latter's rhythmic innovations) remain a vital force in all music. These, together with the atmospheric, instrumental, and dramatic techniques developed by Weber, Berlioz, Liszt, and Wagner constitute the basic resources of most "modern" composers.

The men themselves are sure to rise again in public favor, if of course never to the fantastic heights they (Wagner above all) once attained. And when they are re-valued in years to come, it well may be that the least influential in his own day, Berlioz, will be honored as the most original and germinal figure of them all.

Liszt, too, is likely to be reappraised for his finest contributions, many of which still are unknown or unappreciated by present-day listeners. Meanwhile, it is mainly his shoddier works that are preserved in the display repertories of virtuosos—along with the equally worn-out warhorses of the other concert idols of his time: pianist Anton Rubinstein (1829–94), and the violinists Nicolò Paganini (1782–1840), Henri Vieuxtemps (1820–81), and Henri Wieniawski (1835–80).

Other, less extreme romanticists, who strove to reconcile the rhetoric of the new age with the grammar and logic of the earlier one, have experienced less extreme shifts in popularity. This is particularly true of Felix Mendelssohn-Bartholdy (1809–47), whose more mawkish pieces are now almost forgotten, while we still find new magic in his best chamber and orchestral works and in the faded but authentic grandeur of *Elijah* and *St. Paul*. This is also true of such song specialists as Karl Loewe (1796–1869) and Robert Franz (1815–92), and, perhaps to some, if a lesser extent, of the more versatile and once far more influential Ludwig Spohr (1784–1859) and Camille Saint-Saëns (1835–1921).

Somewhere between the world-shaking epics and the intimate lyric writings of this age lies the bulk of its most substantial achievements in wide musical appeal. Much of this was in the field of opera, whose repertory even today is drawn mainly from the nineteenth century. The list of notables here is so long that I can scarcely do more than run hurriedly through the outstanding names.

In Italy they were led by that great post-Mozartean Gioacchino Rossini (1792–1868); included Gaetano Donizetti (1797–1848), Vincenzo Bellini (1801–35), and Amilcare Ponchielli (1834–86); and were crowned by the greatest purely operatic composer of all time, Giuseppe Verdi (1813–1901), the genius spokesman of both vulgarity and grandeur, who climaxed a long and ceaselessly developing career with the paired triumphs of a true giant: *Otello* and *Falstaff*.

In France they included some of the most distinctive creators of comic and grand opera, and ballet as well. The extraordinary Giacomo Meyerbeer (1791–1864) has suffered a worse fate than that of the ultraromantics, but others whose works still command the delight of present-day listeners were Daniel Auber (1782–1871), Jules Halévy (1799–1862), Ambroise Thomas (1811–96), Charles Gounod (1818–93), Jacques Offenbach (1819–80), Charles Lecocq (1832–1918), Léo Delibes (1836–91), Georges Bizet (1838–75), Jules Massenet (1842–1912), and Robert Planquette (1848–1903). Some of these were frankly "light" composers, but our own relish of their piquancy has brought about a real revival of many of their vivacious works.

In Germany, probably as a result of the imperious domination of first Weber and then Wagner, few operatic composers retain more than a toe-hold in the current international repertory: Heinrich Marschner (1795–1861), Albert Lortzing (1801–51), Carl Nicolai (1810–49), and Friedrich von Flotow (1812–83). Elsewhere the outstanding name is that of a Russian, Michael Glinka (1801–57), who brings us directly to a consideration of the "nationalists" who provided some of the most characteristic achievments of the last part of the century.

The most famous of these schools was that of Glinka's spiritual sons, the Russian "Five": Mili Balakirev (1837–1910), Alexander Borodin (1833–87), Modest Mussorgsky (1839–81), Nikolai Rimsky-Korsakov (1844–1908), and César Cui (1835–1918). Like the *camerata* of 1600, this group was formed by musical amateurs, but unlike the ineffectual Florentines, at least three of the Russians left profound, uneradicable marks on the music of their own and later times. Rimsky-Korsakov perhaps had the most obvious influence, particularly on the glittering exoticism of most later ballet music. But it was Borodin who probably best carried on the Glinka tradition. And it certainly was the awkward, almost inarticulate Mussorgsky who revealed psychological insights deeper than any ultraromantic ever dreamed of, and who today must be considered the true pioneer of "modern" music.

Akin to and influenced by the Russians in many respects, yet distinctively Gallic in their greater lucidity and animation, were some of the Frenchmen mentioned earlier. To them now should be added the still far from appreciated Emanuel Chabrier (1841–94), the supreme stylist Gabriel Fauré (1845–1924), and his more specialized fellow master of the chanson Henri Duparc (1845–1933).

The Czech school led by Bedřich Smetana (1824–84) and Antonin Dvořák (1841–1904) was generally more conservative, but also richly substantial in its contributions to many forms of musical expression—comparatively few of which still are widely known and appreciated outside their own country.

The other early nationalist schools numbered only comparatively minor—if oftentimes ingratiating— figures: Edvard Grieg (1843–1907), best-known of a host of Scandinavians, some of whom only now are being belatedly rescued from merely parochial fame; Juan Arriaga y Balzola (1806–26), forerunner of the later Spanish school; the popular minstrel Stephen Foster (1826–64), and the piano virtuoso Louis Moreau Gottschalk (1829–69), who now seem to have been the major early contributors to a distinctively American music.

There were other men, of course, who fit less conveniently into general classification schemes, though they too embody (if less strikingly) many of the positive or negative tendencies of their time. Outstanding among these were Peter Ilich Tchaikovsky (1840–93), Johannes Brahms (1833–97), and Anton Bruckner (1824–96).

The Russian was disdained by some of his compatriots as unduly subject to German influence, and among sophisticates he is out of favor today for what seem like obvious ultraromantic weaknesses. But now we can realize how authentically Russian he really was and what an immeasurable debt later ballet music in particular owes to his superb sense of theatrical musical effectiveness.

Brahms, too, was disdained, but also acclaimed, during his own lifetime as a "reactionary." Then, in the growing revolt against ultraromanticism, he rose to special fame as a belated classicist, heir to the mantle of Beethoven. Yet today it probably is his plainly romantic lyricism, rather than the grand architecture he labored so hard with, that maintains his widespread popularity.

Similarly, Bruckner, long suffering from his idolaters' obsession for linking him with the entirely different Mahler, is coming to be esteemed less as the post-Wagnerian he himself aspired to be than as a great natural melodist in the Schubertian line of succession.

We can pass more quickly over the Germans Karl Goldmark (1830–1915) and Max Bruch (1838–1920), the Frenchman Édouard Lalo (1823–92), and perhaps even the Belgian César Franck (1822–90), for out of their large repertories only a few exceptionally felicitous works (by Franck in particular) remain in general currency. But we can't ignore the frankly "light" music of this time. Franz von Suppé (1819–95) now is remembered largely by his brash overtures alone, and Emile Waldteufel (1837–1915) only by his coarse-grained waltz-tunes; but the great school of Viennese dance music still contributes incalculably to present-day sensibilities.

Inspired by Haydn, Mozart, and Schubert, this school was founded by Joseph Lanner (1801–43) and Johann Strauss I (1804–49), and brought to its full glory by Johann II (1825–99) and his scarcely less gifted brothers, Josef (1827–70) and Eduard (1835–1916). These men's unpretentious but contagiously "singing" works—operettas, as well as polkas, galops, and waltz-poems—strike many of us today as in some respects the purest musical expression of romanticism. As, for that matter, the Victorian age in England puts on the brightest of its many faces in the sprightly operettas, mostly to Gilbert's librettos, of Sir Arthur Sullivan (1842–1900).

There was a seamier side to the glorious fabric of the nineteenth century. Most of its musicians ignored or disdained the treasures of earlier times (Mendelssohn was one of the few noble exceptions), and some of them labored diabolically to expunge the whole musical past and substitute bowdlerized, adulterated "editions" more in keeping with their own historically perverted philosophies.

Worst of all, even the greatest nineteenth-century composers seemed to have won their Faustian power at the price of an almost complete exhaustion of available expressive resources. Their contemporaries and successors were forced to work under such tremendous technical and psychological handicaps that it is hardly surprising that some of them were driven to intolerable extremes, or that many of them never had the courage to escape from the strictest bonds of then fashionable orthodoxy.

Richard Strauss (1864–1949), for example, stretched to their limit the techniques of Berlioz, Liszt, and Wagner in programmatic orchestral writing, those of Schumann and Brahms in lieder, and those of the whole Viennese tradition at its ripest in the opera *Der Rosenkavalier*.

Gustav Mahler (1860–1911) endeavored frantically to inflate the symphonic apparatus to even more grandiose dimensions. Still idolized by a fanatical band of cultists, these products of his almost insanely ambitious genius strike most of us nowadays as far less genuinely "great" than the same man's simpler, more deeply heartfelt, and far more moving songs and symphonic song-cycles.

Hugo Wolf (1860–1903) had more reliable instincts, for he confined his no less extraordinary gifts almost exclusively to bringing the lied form to a perfection and sharpness of sensibility surpassing anything achieved before or since in blended music and poetry.

Others require no more than enumeration here: Émile Reznicek (1860–1945), Max Reger (1873–1916), Hans Pfitzner (1869–1949), and Engelbert Humperdinck (1854–

1921) in Germany; the Czechs Leoš Janáček (1854–1928) and Josef Suk (1874–1935); the Frenchmen Vincent d'Indy (1851–1931), André Messager (1853–1929), Ernest Chausson (1855–99), Gabriel Pierné (1863–1937), Paul Dukas (1865–1935), and Reynaldo Hahn (1875–1947); the first big names in the belated Spanish nationalistic school, Isaac Albéniz (1860–1909) and Enrique Granados (1867–1916); the generation of Italian operatic composers, led by the apostles of *verismo* (realism), Ruggiero Leoncavallo (1858–1919) and Pietro Mascagni (1863–1945), but also including Arrigo Boïto (1842–1918), Francesco Cilea (1866–1950), Umberto Giordano (1867–1948), Ermanno Wolf-Ferrari (1875–1948), and Riccardo Zandonai (1883–1944), and culminating with the greatest master of post-Wagnerian, post-Verdian musico-dramatic persuasiveness, Giacomo Puccini (1858–1924).

Finally, there were the Russians Michael Ippolitov-Ivanov (1859–1935), Anton Arensky (1861–1906), and Sergei I. Taneiev (1856–1915); the Brahmsian but still distinctively British Sir Edward Elgar (1857–1934); and the first even moderately widely known American, Edward MacDowell (1861–1908), whose strong German and Scandinavian accents, however, now begin to seem far less characteristically native than the authentic twangs of two more obscure men, sure to become better known: Arthur Foote (1853–1937) and Henry Gilbert (1868–1928).

14. *"In My End Is My Beginning"*

> *Lord, we know what we are, but know not what we may be.*
> —SHAKESPEARE: *Hamlet*

WHILE music certainly experienced some kind of major crisis in the twentieth century, it is debatable whether this was any true revolution, and it's even more questionable that the real turning-point was reached early in the 1900's, as "appreciation" books have led many listeners to believe. It is much more likely that the most decisive changes occurred around World War I, after a turbulent transitional period, and that the final break was with the near past only—a counterrevolution, indeed, that restored a lost or twisted continuity with traditions far older than those of the nineteenth century itself.

Nowadays it must be obvious that such "revolutionists" as Richard Strauss and Mahler were essentially post-Wagnerian superromantics endeavoring desperately to recapture earlier romanticism's dramatic impact on listeners' imaginations. And it now seems increasingly probable that their more conservative colleagues were less their opponents than mirror-image twins—romanticists endeavoring no less desperately to re-enliven an earlier "classicism."

Even what seemed around the turn of the century to be so startlingly "new" a style as that of *impressionism* now seems merely a variant of romanticism—more economical, to be sure, and in its quieter way perhaps more effective, but equally limited, and in the long run even less suited to withstand the ever-changing climate of public taste. Brief as its life was, however, more authentic masterpieces were written in this style than in any of the others of its own time. In its emphasis on subtler tone colors and more idiosyncratic forms, and in its attempt to play on the subconscious feelings (rather than the raw emotions) of its listeners, impressionism served as a valuable corrective to the vehement excesses of other post-romantic tendencies, while at the same time it broke paths for the later movements toward music even more directly concerned with "pure" sound-weaving.

The first great name of the new century was that of Claude-Achille Debussy (1862–1918), and the first impressionist masterpiece was his opera *Pelléas et Mélisande*, introduced in 1902. Yet even this well-nigh perfect example exhibits the basic weaknesses of impressionism, particularly an ultrarefinement that for all its atmospheric enchantment often seems overly precious to a more realistic generation. In general it has been Debussy's depictive orchestral and piano works, and perhaps his songs above all, that have maintained his vital place in contemporary musical experience.

Maurice Ravel (1875–1937) usually is ranked close beside Debussy, but he was far more of a true classicist in temperament, and his blend of impressionism with the earlier *style galant* seems more likely to withstand the ravages of time. At the least, he seems sure to rank with such rare composers as Domenico Scarlatti as a transcendental "minor" artist who eventually may loom larger in history than many more obviously "major" colleagues.

The other most distinctive new trend inevitably was called (as a polar opposite of impressionism) "expressionism." *Abstractionism*, however, probably is a more accurate term, though "atonality" was used—quite incorrectly—for a time, and later proponents of this style now speak of themselves as practicing a (or *the*) *twelve-tone technique*.

Ferruccio Busoni (1866–1924) is sometimes hailed as the spiritual father of this school, but its real founder and master was Arnold Schoenberg (1874–1951), who began as a post-Wagnerian romanticist of the most emotional kind, but soon switched to the highly intellectualized, abstract style with which his name now is most closely associated. Yet even in his most rigorous works and for all their unintelligibility for most listeners, Schoenberg still reveals a lingering touch of ultraromanticism. And this is also partly true of his principal followers, Anton von Webern (1883–1945) and Alban Berg (1885–1935). The latter, in particular, though little known to the general public during his lifetime, recently has come to exert a potent influence on the younger composers—and listeners—of today.

Many other composers worked partly between and partly aside from these two main movements of early twentieth-century music. Among the older men, the most important names probably are those of Alexander Scriabin (1872–

1915), Frederick Delius (1862–1934), and Jean Sibelius (1865–   ). These three had little if anything in common, but each illustrates a different variety of the backward or sideways-looking urges.

Scriabin was a self-acclaimed revolutionist with fantastic theories, but beneath their trappings of bogus mysticism, his highfalutin, "ecstatic" big works proved to be nothing but ultraromanticism *in extremis*. They had a short vogue, but only his less pretentious piano works show any real indications of survival power.

Delius is an even stranger case, for though his music is almost static rhythmically and depends almost entirely on its atmospheric effectiveness, his vogue has grown steadily. His appeal is largely extra-musical, hence most powerful to listeners of literary rather than strictly musical temperaments. Yet probably no other composer ever has worked comparable magic with such limited means.

Sibelius is much easier to place and understand, though here again the basic issues often are confused by his devoted cultists. His works are neo-Brahmsian, neo-Tchaikoskyan, in almost completely orthodox nineteenth-century style. Their great popularity seems to depend largely on the new public's admiration for a "grand manner" allied neither with the aural harshness of the abstractionists nor with the tenuous, "soft-focus" effects commonly associated with (though by no means completely characteristic of) the impressionists.

In general, the lesser figures do not depart far from the general tendencies of the times, though of course many of them reveal considerable individuality in sometimes highly distinctive works.

In France, Gustave Charpentier (1860–   ) is chiefly noted for his "naturalistic" opera *Louise*, Erik Satie (1866– 1925) as an eccentric stimulator of the later Parisian *"Six,"* Albert Roussel (1869–1937) as a middleman between the impressionists and the more classic-minded followers of Vincent d'Indy. In Russia, the conservative nationalists include Alexander Glazunov (1865–1936), Reinhold Glière

(1875–   ), Basil Kalinnikov (1866–1901), Nikolai Medtner (1879–1951), Nikolai Miaskovsky (1881–1950), and the great pianist Serge Rachmaninoff (1873–1943)—a major, if belated, romantic composer, whose lush emotionalism remains as irresistible to some tastes as it is abhorrently overripe to others.

Elsewhere in Europe there are the quasi-impressionistic Spanish nationalists Manuel de Falla (1876–1946) and Joaquín Turina (1882–1949); the Hungarian and Romanian neo-classicists Ernest Dohnányi (1877–   ) and Georges Enesco (1881–   ); Gian Franscesco Malipiero (1882–   ) and Ottorino Respighi (1879–1936) of Italy; the Dane Carl Nielsen (1865–1931); the Czech Jaromir Weinberger (1896–   ); and the Swiss-American Ernest Bloch (1880–   ). A post-Elgarian British school includes Gustave Holst (1874–1934), Arnold Bax (1883–   ), and, most importantly, Ralph Vaughan Williams (1872–   ). And in America we have the traditionalists John Alden Carpenter (1876–1951) and Howard Hansen (1896–   ), the Australian-born folklorist Percy Grainger (1882–   ), the impressionist Charles Griffes (1884–1920), and others—of whom the most striking by far is the ruggedly individualistic, "prematurely modernistic" Charles Ives (1874–   ).

But for the most part all these men are somewhat outside the mainstreams of historical developments. And so are such masters of light music in the Straussian tradition as Franz Lehár (1870–1948) and Oskar Straus (1870–   ); the not-dissimilar exponent of popular British entertainment, Eric Coates (1886–   ); and, in America, Jerome Kern (1885–1945) and Sigmund Romberg (1887–   ).

CONTEMPORARY MAINSTREAMS

The second quarter of the century has seen the movement begun by Schoenberg widening in influence. A few composers, like Ernest Křenek (1900–   ), for example, now write exclusively in this style, but more and more younger men are making use of the twelve-tone technique at least to some extent. Perhaps, with many other streams stemming from various sources, this is gradually being incorporated into a mainstream for which the only all-inclusive name is *eclecticism*. Its diverse beginnings (abstractionism, neo-classicism, "realism," etc.) were primarily reactionary movements —against impressionism, grandiosity, nationalism, and every other form of romanticism—but it soon lost many of its extremist, "futuristic" elements. Now it seems to have settled down into a more or less homogeneous style (or variety of styles), which eventually may be considered a twentieth-century "classicism," in which the influence of baroque and even medieval traditions are evident even under the stiff mask of modern "objectivity."

One important element is the *Gebrauchsmusik* (workaday music, or music "for use") associated first with a group of young German composers led by Paul Hindemith (1895–   ). Other significant contributions stem from the Parisian *"Six,"* who worked more as individuals than as a closely allied school. Darius Milhaud (1892–   ) and the Swiss Arthur Honegger (1892–   ) are the most important of these, but they have written in many styles and forms, and it probably is the lesser figures of Francis Poulenc (1899–   ) and Georges Auric (1899–   ) who represent more characteristically the early reputation of *Les Six* for sardonic wit and the half-ironical, half-admiring use of music-hall and other popular materials.

More influential than any of these men are three never (or not for long) confined to a single school or trend, who must be considered the outstanding spokesmen of eclecticism if not of the whole first half of this century: Béla Bartók (1881–1945), Serge Prokofiev (1891–1953), and Igor Stravinsky (1882–   ).

Bartók—along with Zoltán Kodály (1882–   )—made his early reputation as a Hungarian folklorist, but soon forged a distinctively personal style all his own, which in his last works lost some of its uncompromising "difficulty" as it gained in breadth of appeal and in nobly dramatic stature.

Prokofiev was an unpredictable, mercurial, and versatile personality, who often baffled his admirers, but whose best works reveal a remarkably daring imagination and uncommonly precise and powerful musicianship. The clarity and point of his writing, and his superb sense of sonority resources, in particular, have strongly influenced nearly all contemporary music.

The influence of Stravinsky has been even stronger, but I should like to postpone momentarily a discussion of his works while I run swiftly through a long list of other notable, if less outstandingly important figures in the music of our own day. Although I group them for convenience by countries, most of them are primarily eclectic in style (or styles), and many of them now are working in the United States, though not necessarily in any characteristically "American" idiom.

In Soviet Russia the leading name is that of the incredibly gifted Dmitri Shostakovich (1906–   ), though it now seems certain he never will fulfill his early promise. Aram Khachaturian (1903–   ) and Dmitri Kabalevsky (1904–   ) are lesser, if highly colorful figures.

In France, where Honegger, Milhaud, and Poulenc still largely dominate the scene, there are the post-impressionist Jacques Ibert (1890–   ), the neo-Scarlattian Jean Françaix (1912–   ), and many men still little known in this country, of whom the most notable seem to be Olivier Messiaen (1908–   ) and Henri Sauguet (1901–   ).

In Great Britain the most important probably are William Walton (1902–   ) and Benjamin Britten (1913–   ), while the lesser figures include Lord Berners (1883–1950), Arthur Bliss (1891–   ), Constant Lambert (1905–51), and that extraordinary, belated Elizabethan, "Peter Warlock" (Philip Heseltine, 1894–1930).

In the United States it is particularly hard for a contemporary and compatriot to select outstanding men with any objective fairness. So after singling out Aaron Copland (1900–   ) for special mention, I'll simply list some more or less arbitrarily chosen others, strictly in order of birth dates: Walter Piston (1894–   ), Roger Sessions (1896–   ), Virgil Thomson (1896–   ), Roy Harris (1898–   ), Samuel Barber (1910–   ), and Jerome Moross (1913–   ). But of course there are many others, including the highly successful dramatic composer Gian-Carlo Menotti (1911–   ), the versatile Leonard Bernstein (1918–   ), and the experimentalists Edgar Varèse (1885–   ), Henry Cowell (1897–   ), John Cage (1912–   ), and Alan Hovhaness (1911–   ), to name just a few.

Better known internationally are the Brazilian Heitor Villa-Lobos (1887–   ), the Mexican Carlos Chávez (1899–   ), the Austrian-born Ernst Toch (1887–   ), the Czech-born Bohuslav Martinů (1890–   ), and the German-born Kurt Weill (1900–50)—who after coming to this country turned his great dramatic talents from *Gebrauchsmusik* to authentically "American" musical comedies and the rapidly growing new school of informal opera.

Perhaps the most important strictly American contributions to music history have been in just these fields of musical comedy and non-grand opera, and in "popular" and dance music. The more ambitious works of George Gershwin (1898–1937) have had an influence that quite transcends whatever may be their æsthetic weaknesses. And in his songs, as in the stage works of Richard Rodgers (1902–   ) and the dance pieces of Duke Ellington (1899–   ), later-day scholars are likely to find a historical "significance" that currently is instinctively realized by the man in the street, who responds irresistibly to their melodic and rhythmic invention.

Impossible as it is to evaluate the achievements of our own time with any true objectivity or to single out one man as summing up the diverse work of all these composers, I can't close my bird's-eye survey without a personal tribute to one composer who many of his contemporaries are confident should be considered, if not the giant, at least the most illuminating spokesman of our age.

For some listeners, Stravinsky is the colorful Rimskyan composer of *L'Oiseau de feu* and *Petrouchka*. For others, he is the naturalistic creator of *Le Sacre* and *Les Noces*. For still others, he is the biting satirist of *L'Histoire du soldat* and the Octet for Winds. And there are many more who find in his later ballets the purest essence of music for the dance.

He is all these—and more. For surely no other contemporary composer has contributed so richly or so provocatively to our over-all musical experience. Yet perhaps no other of any age has hewn more closely to the logical line of his own development, regardless of the popular pressure to repeat earlier successes. And at his greatest—in the mighty *Œdipus Rex*, the profoundly tender *Orpheus*, and the triumphant affirmation of the *Symphonie de psaumes*—Stravinsky brings the matured powers of artistic philosophy to battle with the darkest forces of the irrationality and despair of our times. The "ecstasy without grimace" and "submission without tears" of these works (in Santayana's unforgettable words) indeed "hold heaven and earth better together—and hold them better apart—than could a mad imagination."

15. Exploring for Our Own Homesteads

> *The history of music can begin with any given present, now, or in the past, to enrich our experience here and now.*
>
> —W. D. ALLEN:
> *Philosophies of Music History*

FEW OF us can resist the heady intoxication of glimpsing for the first time the whole world of music lying like a Promised Land at our feet. Yet once we actually begin to explore its immensities, we find that the life of a pioneer involves sobering hardships as well as exciting hopes. Many of the mountain peaks that beckoned so invitingly in our birds-eye view prove to be well-nigh inaccessible, and whenever we pause in their laborious ascent, we recall with increasing nostalgia the comforts of our former, less adventurous, but also less exhausting life.

It's great fun, in the first flush of enthusiasm, to run through record catalogues, checking dozens of composers of all ages you want to know better. But as you settle down to listen to the works picked out with such anticipation, they sometimes prove to be sadly disappointing on first acquaintance. And then you're only too ready to turn back to the easier and more thrilling splendors of a familiar Tchaikovskyan or Brahmsian favorite.

Of course, not all your ventures into unfamiliar new or old repertories are likely to be so unsuccessful. But certainly not all of your first steps off the beaten paths will seem to be immediately rewarding. And whether you blame me or some other writer for making exaggerated claims, or blame yourself for lacking powers of wide discrimination, the usual result is that your brave resolutions are weakened, even if you don't entirely abandon your dream of building up a truly comprehensive record library.

Youngsters, with their omnivorous appetites and as yet unformed tastes, seldom run into this kind of impasse. Avid for any and every new kind of experience, they usually are undisturbed by meeting a work that momentarily baffles or displeases them. But for older listeners, especially those more or less set in their tastes, this problem of effectively widening musical horizons is a very practical and serious one.

For whatever encouragement it's worth, I can only assure you that this predicament is neither uncommon nor hopeless. You have simply tried to go too far and too fast. Successful explorations don't gamble on leaping blindly into unknown territory. They demand a carefully planned, step-by-step approach, with frequent pauses for rest and for establishing a strong base for the next advance.

The essential first step is to know exactly where you're starting *from:* just what music, composers, and periods do you now find most congenial? The next is to plan an organized campaign to extend the boundaries of this familiar territory, progressing always along the lines of least resistance.

In any panoramic survey of music history, the most natural direction of movement is from the past to the present. But in artistic experience itself, where the far past and current experimentation usually present the greatest difficulties, the easiest progression almost always is radially outward from your given starting-point. Generally, then, a *reverse* chronological direction—moving backward rather than forward in time—is the simplest to take. Certain jumps, however, may capitalize advantageously on the fact that one age tends to react more or less violently against the characteristic trends of the one immediately preceding, while it shares to some extent ideals dominant in the age before that.

Of course, such era-affinities are only loosely effective. The feeling of affinity for certain individual composers usually transcends chronology. And this gives us another valuable means of extending our personal scope by moving from one period to another by way of such seemingly timeless and universally appealing "steppingstones."

Many of the giants (Bach, Mozart, and Beethoven, for obvious examples) are so limitless in their scope that any one of them provides almost infinite room for the expansion of your own experience. Paradoxical as it may seem, specialization, at least for a time, often is a requisite for comprehensiveness. Thoroughly studying one many-faceted personality, we learn to trace the development of expressive means throughout his own growth and in many diverse forms and media. From that point, any one of these forms or media may serve as a steppingstone to the better understanding of other composers who make use of it as a means of expression of their own quite different personalities.

In short, the highroad to musical catholicity—as to that in all fields of human knowledge—is to work always from the well known through some intermediate common ground into what is less familiar, and never to leap unprepared into the completely unknown.

It has probably struck you that this "progress by affinities" is closely similar to "working with the grain of one's temperament," suggested earlier in these pages. The method is indeed much the same, but your own motivation is likely to have changed significantly. Earlier, you tended to follow your ears in seeking whatever enjoyment you knew and relished best. Now, better oriented in the whole history and world of music, you are deliberately searching for larger periods or fields where you have the best chance of soon learning to feel at home. You still can't cross your instinctive taste-reactions, but you have come to realize far better how they can be exploited, extended, and developed.

The great secret, I believe, is learning to reconcile the conflict between what we think we *should* enjoy and what we actually *do* enjoy. Happiness is impossible as long as our common practice contradicts our ideals. And tolerance, as well as charity, begins at home. In music, as elsewhere, neither the determined pursuit of an entirely impracticable ideal nor the lazy acceptance of purely pragmatic pleasure can long or deeply satisfy any normal listener. All work and all play are alike in making Jack a very discontented as well as a dull boy. Each of us must learn for himself the best proportions in which work and play can be mixed— and separated.

But now let us see how some of these methods and principles can be applied by a listener whose special favorites at present are, say, romantic piano concertos. The logical first step is not into some entirely new field, but in deepening his knowledge of this one: going on from Tchaikovsky's First Concerto, for example, to the same composer's Second; from those by Schumann and Grieg to Chopin's, Liszt's, and Brahms's; and later perhaps to Weber's *Konzertstück* and the seldom heard piano concertos by Dvořák, Rubinstein, and Rimsky-Korsakov.

Then, from this firmly established beachhead, it is possible to make probing explorations in various directions: expanding acquaintance with composers already known by going on to their many works for piano or orchestra alone, or investigating earlier and later developments of the piano-concerto form itself—backward to those by Beethoven, Mozart, and Bach, and forward to those by, say, Franck, Rachmaninoff, Scriabin, Ravel, and Prokofiev. Or the listener might move to concertos for violin or other instruments—at first, of course, to those by already well-known composers. But as a rule he'll find it easier to stick for a while longer to a keyboard instrument and orchestra, together or separately. One easy avenue is to compare a Mozart or Bach concerto first known in a piano version with the same work as performed with a harpsichord in the solo role. From these he can go on to unfamiliar harpsichord concertos and even to the more popular rococo and baroque pieces for harpsichord solo. And from Couperin and Domenico Scarlatti he'll find it surprisingly natural to jump far forward in time to the piano solos of Debussy, Ravel, and Poulenc.

This kind of "beachhead, exploration, and consolidation" approach obviously can be utilized with any other musical form or medium. But wherever the exploring listener ventures, he never should fail, as soon as his interest begins to flag, to return to his old favorites—both for relaxation and for the thrill of making fresh discoveries in long-familiar works. For one of the greatest rewards of exploration is that you not only find new music to enjoy, but also find new enjoyment in the music you've known before. It hasn't changed, of course, but with each change in your own perspective, long-familiar music reveals unfamiliar facets.

Indeed, the goal of all exploration well may be:

> . . . to arrive where we started
> And know the place for the first time.

In any case, few of us have the insatiable curiosity (or perhaps the nervous restlessness) for a whole life or even many years devoted primarily to exploration and adventure. Sooner or later most of us tend to settle down in some kind of home-place—and in music we generally end by listening

mainly to the works of a few especially congenial composers
or to those written in one favorite medium or several closely
allied media.

Educators, professional musicians, and truly catholic listeners usually sneer at the cruder manifestations of this
kind of specialization: at opera devotees who have little
interest in symphonic music, say, or singlehearted enthusi-
asts for piano music only. Certainly, narrow restrictions of
taste severely limit the potential growth of one's experience.
Nevertheless, even a small field is as much as some listeners
want to (or can) cultivate. And all of us are limited to some
extent (by our temperaments, by available time and energy,
and by many other factors), so the significant question is
not the actual size of our special field, but whether it gives
us ample living-space for our individual natures.

Whatever our needs, they never can be met by impressively titled recordings that sit unheard on our shelves.
Nor can any genuine urge for an expanded musical scope
be satisfied by a bare smattering of diverse historical samples. Useful as anthologies may be in institutional record-
collections, they generally are too fragmentary to contribute
vitally to our individual musical growth. The best disc
anthologies are rich in helpful leads when we are exploring
entirely new territories, but for lasting satisfaction we eventually have to build up our own collection to represent more
completely the kind or kinds of music that mean most to us.

Our personal record libraries must be evaluated less on
their comprehensiveness as such than on the richness and
variety of detail within a framework whose size and contour
are shaped to fit ourselves alone. The catholic listener will
have a catholic library, the specialist a specialized one. The
prime value of either depends on how completely the music
itself—whatever it may be—has been absorbed into vital
experience.

◇◇
◇◇

PART III

One World—Many Mansions

16. Breaking the Bias Barriers

> . . . thus do we of wisdom and of reach,
> With windlasses and with assays of bias,
> By indirections find directions out.
> —SHAKESPEARE: Hamlet

LIKE a castaway washed up on the beach of a tropical paradise, the novice listener enters his newly discovered musical worlds in a delirium of mingled ecstasy and fear. Tentatively tasting the enticing but suspect fruits spread so profusely before him, he dares trust, at first, only a few that best meet his pragmatic tests for safe enjoyment. And for long he seldom dares venture far from the narrow circle of his initial camp.

But even the carefree delights of beachcombing pall in time. Sooner or later, boldly or reluctantly, our Crusoe begins to think beyond the present moment and the next meal. Eventually he is driven to explore the full extent and resources of his new world, to seek a wider range of both activity and food, and to locate a true homesite.

It is somewhat the pattern of a novice's normal musical development that I have sketched so far. Part I of this book has dealt with the listener's instinctive tastes and discoveries. Then, in Part II, I have suggested a means by which maturing listeners can orient themselves in music history and survey more systematically the incalculable treasures that are available, if not always easily accessible.

Each of these two general types of musical approach has obvious rewards. Yet for many listeners the excessive self-centeredness of the former eventually becomes irksome, while the latter seems to make demands that often are impracticable if not entirely impossible to meet. The problem at this stage plainly is how we can best reconcile these different, often contradictory approaches.

The following chapters enlarge in more detail a solution suggested in the last chapter: the intensive cultivation of whatever specific musical region each of us selects for himself—instinctively or rationally—as the most congenial tonal "home-place" in which to live, work, play, and grow. But even though this involves the selection of one or more limited areas for settlement, it should not imply that their boundaries are immutably fixed. We do not have to feel fenced in unless we want to—there are people who depend on walls for a sense of security. When we need to expand, new fields stretch out on every side. And one of the purposes of the following area-studies will be to chart the directions in which expansion into adjacent territories may be most easily achieved.

As you may have learned for yourself, any realm of art possesses a peculiar, Einsteinian, fourth-dimensional topography. What chronologically and geographically is right next door may be incredibly distant as measured by the rubber yardstick of musical "affinities." On the other hand, spirits who are our closest temperamental kin well may be composers from locales and ages that quite literally are "far away and long ago."

Æsthetically, then, all music is one world. But, unfortunately, few of us are equipped for full citizenship in this far-flung commonwealth. Our backgrounds, our unfamiliarity with "foreign" languages and cultures, and, above all, our own temperamental quirks often impose harsh practical limitations on our theoretical freedom of movement and insight. Fatal as it is to acquiesce passively in these limitations, to ignore their existence is stupidly naïve. Comfortably protecting or intolerably confining, the barriers always are there. And whether we hope to conceal them or burst gateways through, they need to be studied and understood.

One barrier, the most massive of all outside the world of music, is our long ingrown aversion to anything unfamiliar and alien. This fear, born in self-consciousness and too often susceptible of growth into hatred, is, of course, a basic cause of most of our social and political conflicts. But in art generally, and perhaps in music particularly, its effect is less powerful and dangerous than elsewhere.

Here, as we have seen, individual tastes tend to override regional and chronological differences. For the normally curious novice, the comparative lack of traditional backgrounds and prejudices is a marked advantage in approaching unfamiliar music. When almost everything you hear is more or less new to you, the exact degree of strangeness seldom is either apparent or crucial. Even after your tastes become more fixed, truly great music possesses such imperious power to penetrate far beneath surface consciousness that the strongest barrier of unfamiliarity seldom can withstand its bold impact.

But of course other types of barriers—divisive forces, perhaps, rather than solid walls—must be reckoned with. Yet while these obviously encourage segregative discriminations where there should be none, they can be transformed— once we understand them—from Iron Curtains into binding links between different musical territories and philosophies.

One of them has been noted earlier: the temperamental distinctions generally described as extravert and introvert. We have seen that while these natural bents may seem initially to impede the development of musical catholicity, they can be advantageously exploited, first to intensify our enjoyment of especially congenial types of music, and eventually even to ease our preliminary approach to other types that originally had seemed forbiddingly alien. And most of us soon learn that these extravert-introvert classifications are complementary as well as contrasting. They represent two equally essential *poles* of human character. Heavily as they may be unbalanced in any individual, no person is wholly dominated by one pole alone, and in many of us both are powerfully influential, if not always to the same degree or at the same time.

I re-emphasize the sometimes ambiguous duality, or ambivalence, of these traits, in order to illuminate the similar nature of two other divisive forces that tend to become increasingly important as our listening assumes greater specialization. One of these is our instinctive general attitude toward *size*—our personal susceptibility to the polar attractions of the big and the miniature. The second is our no less innate bias for or against instrumental as opposed to vocal music.

The former operates in all regions of art and life, but usually so subconsciously that few of us are aware, until it it specifically drawn to our attention, how profoundly it shapes our tastes and judgments. Normally, indeed, it is buried so deeply that we fall into the most dangerous trap that all biases lay for us: our own way of thinking seems so natural and convincing that we simply cannot comprehend how someone else may hold with equally assured conviction a seemingly diametrically opposed point of view.

If our propensity is for grandeur, we instinctively tend to deprecate small-scale works no matter how nearly perfect they may be of their kind. Quantity as well as quality figures significantly in our judgments, and for us, like boxing experts, it is an almost automatic assumption that "a good big man must beat a good little man." On the other hand, if our prime criteria are immaculate purity of conception and perfect craftsmanship of execution, we are likely to find most "big" works disturbingly uneven in both respects.

In either case, an arbitrary standard of ideal size denies or distorts the worth of everything that falls outside our inelastic specifications. We forget that art is not sport nor even craftsmanship alone, that masterpieces are not competitive, that every work of art is sufficient unto itself.

Probably we cannot—and perhaps should not try to—change our basic bias: instinctively our imaginations will always respond more zestfully to works exemplifying one or the other extreme of the scale. But that should never commit us to denying stubbornly the evident worth and appeal of music at the other extreme.

The second kind of bias is perhaps unique to music. More singular, perhaps even more powerful, than the others, it accounts for the seemingly compulsive orientation of most listeners in response to the magnetic attractions of the human voice at one pole and of instruments at the other. Such leanings long have been scorned by professional musicians and educators, who often indignantly deny that any such cross-pull actually exists. Music is music, whether sung or played, or both. Only a tonal ignoramus "likes" orchestral works "better" than lieder, say, or an opera "better" than a string quartet!

They're absolutely right, of course—in theory. Nevertheless, most listeners cherish such irrational preferences of medium. We generally make certain exceptions to our usual rule, and only the most naïve novices are likely to make a candid admission of their basic vocal-instrumental bias. But few of us are entirely free from—or unaware of—this prejudice.

It is so widespread and deep-rooted, indeed, that attempts to deal with it on a purely rational basis seldom have any real success. I believe that the source of its certainly irrational and usually ignorant surface manifestations is a fundamental warp of the whole personality. It took me a good many years to arrive at this view, but I am at last willing to concede that even the most experienced listener is likely in his heart to give precedence either to instruments or to voices. He will never express it with a novice's crudeness, or claim to like one better than the other, but there always will be something in him that responds to them in different ways and that—given any encouragement at all—tends to cherish one just a bit more dearly than the other.

With all these personality biases, the supreme danger lies in the childishly blind insistence on maintaining one attraction in direct opposition to another. For our response to the complementary (rather than antithetical) pulls of magnetic poles never can be a simple reaction. Such forces are not subject to arithmetical addition and cancellation, but to what mathematicians call the "algebraic sum of two vectors"—a complex process in which both the magnitude and the angles of the two forces must be taken into account. In more humanistic terms, what we must learn is to hold fast to Jung's reminder that there may be in two related but commonly severed views "a common living something which, shimmering multi-colored in the soul, combines and sanctions both."

Unrecognized, misunderstood, or uncontrolled, our ingrained biases effectively seal us within a narrow prison cell of tolerance and taste, outside which we can find little pleasure, and less comprehension of those who have freed themselves from such bonds. But under sympathetic control, even these fundamental warps may be turned to the notable enhancement of both our specialized enjoyments and our whole range of musical experience.

Even before we explore some of the means of such exploitation, the mere bringing of our prejudices out of their submerged depths into the light of conscious study helps immeasurably in developing keener insights into ourselves, and into the various types of music we are likely to encounter, whether with predisposed sympathy or antipathy. Once we have sound reasons for the otherwise inexplicable vagaries of our tastes, *why* and *how* we like or dislike certain works becomes far more meaningful than the plain likes or dislikes themselves.

Most significantly, the biases indicate the general direction in which our individual temperaments are "grained"— the direction in which we best begin to work, and indeed always will work most effectively. And perhaps nowhere is the ability of "working with the grain" more useful than in learning how our sense of active *participation* in the works we enjoy most can be stretched to operate first in larger and eventually in alien areas.

17. The Participating Listener

> *In music, more than in any other branch of art, understanding is given only to those who make an active effort. Passive receptivity is not enough.*
> —STRAVINSKY: *Chronicle of My Life*

WHEN music educators finally awoke to the disconcerting realization that the phonograph and radio were something more than ingenious toys, no potentiality of the anticipated Mechanized Dark Ages horrified them more than the possibility of "canned" music's ousting "live" performances as the main medium of listening experience.

Yet now, when that dreaded fate actually has come to pass, even the more hidebound educators are forced to concede that most of their dire prophecies have proved baseless. Opening Euterpe's sacred books to the "rabble," even at second hand, obviously has done Euterpe less harm than it has done the rabble good. The lowest common denominator of taste now is operative on an immensely larger scale, to be sure, but an amazingly large minority of the musically illiterate have demonstrated an allegiance to æsthetic standards certainly equal, if not superior, to those of "connoisseur" audiences of the past. And in their contributions to repertory expansion, to the establishment of more rigorous criteria of interpretative techniques, and to the general growth of interest in "good" music, the phonograph and radio plainly have outweighed those of the contemporary concert hall and opera house.

One dread demon, however, has never been completely exorcised, but remains to shadow the optimism of the new listening public itself: the apparent abandonment of intimate, trained, and active *participation* in music-making. Serious "art" music in the past was addressed primarily to hearers who either were performers themselves, amateur if not professional, or at least were musically well read and experienced. Nowadays, however, the great majority of listeners not only cannot sing or play themselves—they cannot even read music.

How is it possible for such literally musical illiterates to listen as intelligently, or even as sympathetically, as properly educated hearers? Can music for the musically ignorant ever be more than a passive, mystifying experience? Aren't they likely to relish most (as Santayana warned) their own surrender to a tonally accompanied "drowsy revery enlivened by nervous thrills"?

These are reasonable questions, which cannot be easily evaded. How deeply they trouble today's listeners is vividly attested by the new musical public's apparently insatiable craving for enlightenment. Like "that heavenly word, Mesopotamia," *appreciation* has come to be a kind of shibboleth or magic password to a sacred inner circle. Like the Ellington dance piece that asserted: "If it ain't got that swing, it don't mean a thing," music surely cannot be truly significant for any listener who ain't got "appreciation."

Well, "appreciation" is so omnipotent a term that it can cover almost every aspect of musical understanding, but unquestionably one of its most vital elements involves some kind of participation in the musical performances we hear. By definition, a listener does not perform, and if he is untrained it is practically impossible for him to project himself imaginatively into a performer's role. Unable to read scores, he cannot "hear" music mentally, from the inside out, as it were, either separately from or simultaneously with physically hearing it from the outside in. And no illiterate listener can afford to delude himself: the joys of direct music-making never can be his, nor can he ever listen with the knowing, professional, analytic ears and mind of the trained executant.

But that is not to say that these limitations are fatal. The music-makers' capacities for direct and indirect participation are not the only or perhaps even the most important requirements for understanding music—and still less for enjoying it. Forget momentarily your own sense of inferiority where technicalities are concerned, and honestly reconsider your own experience. Whatever your resources, haven't you been convinced on some occasions that you were exercising them to your full ability and that you were deriving the maximum musical satisfaction of which you were capable? Or, at least, isn't there a clear distinction in your own mind between frankly passive listening, letting the music pour in one ear and out the other, and a very different kind, in which your whole organism is alert to capture and respond to every note and every inflection of what you hear?

The word "participation," after all, means "to partake" and "to share" as well as "to take part in." Formal training certainly enables you to know more *about* what you hear. It simplifies the task of intelligent perception by providing convenient terminologies and frames of reference. But actively participatory listening always demands something more: an enlivened sense not only of alert receptivity but of eager reaching out toward the object of attention.

It never is enough for the work alone to come to life. You must come fully and intensely alive yourself to seize your full share of it. As Beethoven once noted, "Only the flint of a man's mind can strike fire in music." And that applies no less to the listener than to the composer and performer.

Listening to music from records in your own home actually has certain marked advantages, to be balanced against the more generally recognized disadvantages, over hearing it from live performances in concert halls and opera houses. These include an enhanced freedom from physical and psychological constraint, fewer distractions to defocus your attention, and, above all, the never fully appreciated privileges of *repetition*—of going back to a faultily grasped section, of isolating different details in each replaying, and of learning even the largest works by rote perhaps, but certainly by heart.

These advantages can be reversed of course, from the point of view of participation, by utilizing them only as listening sedatives rather than stimulants. Any environment is favorable only as you make it so. For some home listeners, effort is confined to flicking an "on" switch before they sit down to wait for music to "come to" them. Such passive listening often has been compared with taking a warm bath in music—a rank injustice, for bathing usually involves at least the bather's taking the trouble to scrub himself!

It is only too easy, too, to mask passivity by a bogus spirit of musical reverence—expressed in the quasi-devotional attitude of "music-lovers" who proclaim their piety by listening with heads bowed and faces modestly shielded. I have always had the sneaking suspicion (invariably confirmed when I aped this attitude myself) that before long they are doing less listening than napping. Actually, closing our eyes merely encourages daydreaming, whereas sitting up alertly, or, better still, striding vigorously around the room, succeeds far better in keeping all the senses (and hearing is not the only one involved in true participation) electrically vitalized.

Even talking or reading while you listen (provided it is directly concerned with the music at hand) may be helpful. When you and a friend compete in spotting significant details of performance or composition, or when program notes prod you into registering otherwise unexpected and unobserved musical points, both your enjoyment and your perceptiveness can be markedly enhanced.

With live concerts, sound films, and telecasts, your eyes can be tremendously stimulating guides for your ears. It is amazing how much more vivid a particular solo or group part seems to sound when you watch the movements and expressions of the players. And though this visual guidance is impossible in phonographic listening, it still may be achieved to some extent in the imagination. Or, if you are active and uninhibited enough, you can make an exciting "kinesthetic substitution" by going through pertinent rhythmical motions or even attempting to shadow-conduct the performance.

Perhaps the eye's greatest helpfulness is in following a printed score simultaneously with listening to performance of the music. Actually *reading* orchestral scores is a complex task even for those literate in simpler piano or vocal notation, but it can be learned with a little sustained effort. Merely *following* the various instrumental parts, however, incomparably stimulates your mind to hear more acutely and to identify and analyze more closely everything it hears. If you begin by reading a score-reading guide and following comparatively simple scores, you can learn more in a few hours of repetitive practice of this kind than you ever can in weeks of strictly theoretical, textbook musical study.

And there is a still simpler, nearly as rewarding way in which your eyes and ears may co-operate in participatory listening. Probably more than half the music ever written involves *words*—either as a text for which the music is a setting, or as a more or less detailed program or plot for instrumental works. Much of the meaning of highly organized patterns of sound alone may be blurred or lost if we comprehend only imperfectly its purely tonal language. But when these are matched to intelligible verbal patterns, the text provides an unmistakable key to the music's significance.

The explanatory process works both ways. Not only do words clarify our understanding of the music, but the latter intensifies and enriches the text. When we learn to grasp both elements simultaneously, not merely as an additive sum, but in a thoroughly blended and transformed whole, we discover in such an integration one of the most profound experiences that music—or any art—can provide.

Here it is essential not only to grasp what the text is about, but also to follow the exact words themselves, which are not always aurally intelligible even when they are sung in English or some other language familiar to you. For in this way you can discover the extent to which composers make expressive use of the actual *sounds*, as well as the sense, of words—sounds which, like any other kind of tonal materials, are colored and shaped by the phrasing and intonation of their singer players.

This, of course, is the fundamental argument against performing vocal works in translations. But that is beside the main point I want to make here: the distinction between merely *preparative* use of a text and its more closely *participatory* use in simultaneous listening to and reading the entire work.

The preparatory reading of a vocal text, "program," or depictive title is valuable, too, but in a quite different way. This *primes* your mind by suggesting the general mood of the music you are about to hear and supplies a kind of ready-made frame of reference for what is to come. Indeed, many listeners depend so heavily on such aids that they feel a distinct sense of insecurity when they approach so-called absolute music, for which no appropriate specific attitudes have been suggested to them, except perhaps in the seldom completely reliable "descriptive" commentaries of annotators.

I shall return later to this problem of "participating" in instrumental music lacking depictive programs or titles. Meanwhile, it is surely apparent that no serious listener can afford to neglect one of the most powerful available weapons for tackling all music with which words are associated in any way. Words may be used merely to set up a congenial listening-response atmosphere. Or, as vocal texts, they can be interfused with the music itself in an integrated experience that carries its own unmistakable meaning. Either way, and to the degree with which they sharpen our insights and bring into play our optimum powers of attention, they make listening far more than mere receptivity.

There are as many ways of listening as there are kinds of music and types of listeners. Each has its place—even the passive immersion in a drugged nirvana or the unobtrusively pleasant background for dining or conversation that is supplied by appropriate tonal "wallpaper."

But let us render unto Muzak that which is Muzak's! While we all may relish these harmless pleasures on occasion, we do not dare claim that they represent any real *listening* enjoyment. And if "participating listening" often involves as much work as it does entertainment, many of us come eventually to cherish its incandescent moments as those in which we feel most fully charged with energy, most closely akin to—and part of—great art, and indeed ourselves most fully and dynamically *alive*.

18. Outward Drama: Opera

> *Opera: an exotic and irrational entertainment.*
> —SAMUEL JOHNSON:
> *Dictionary of the English Language*

NOWHERE in music is listener participation easier, more importunate indeed, than in opera. In the opera house itself you are simultaneously listener, spectator, and emotional participant in the multiformed dramatic action on the stage and in the orchestra pit. But even in phonographic performances the meaning of everything you hear in words and tones is primarily intelligible and moving as an audible evocation of the invisible drama.

Obviously, the better you know the story and the more vividly you can picture some appropriate spectacle, the more specific your sense of participation becomes. Yet even without detailed knowledge of actual stage productions, you find that action and characterization are so powerfully implied in the music itself that you are almost forced to create some kind of imaginatively plausible settings and actors for it. These non-musical aspects of what you hear perhaps can be suppressed by a deliberate effort of the will, but if you do strain in this way to listen to the music for its own sake, you are likely to realize that what is left is neither purified nor entirely self-sufficient. The essence of this music lies in its overtly dramatic quality. While many parts of it may make perfectly good tonal sense when heard objectively, the work as a whole rarely can be more than a pallid ghost of its full-blooded, frankly sensual true life.

This, I am sure, accounts for a singular cleavage in listeners' attitudes toward opera. To those willing to accept opera in its totality, it provides unparalleled entertainment, musically and otherwise. But to those who stubbornly resist its enticements to full participation, it almost invariably remains an unsatisfactory, perhaps tawdry, and certainly frustratingly incomplete experience.

In any case, the power to inflame both love and hate is characteristic of opera's supremely paradoxical nature. It is a mélange of many arts and techniques—yet the whole always is greater than the sum of its parts. Throughout history, opera has been the darling of the masses or (sometimes *and*) the pet of aristocratic, moneyed, or fashionable minorities. And while in many ways it is the freest and most catholic of forms, it also is the one that embodies the most rigid and artificial conventions.

Perhaps the key to the enjoyment of opera is simply the unquestioning acceptance of these conventions. Certainly nothing else in all music depends more completely on the "willing suspension of disbelief." The greatest of all operatic paradoxes is that its only too obvious weaknesses are its basic strengths.

Rationally considered, it surely is plain enough that "to produce a dragon, to describe a dragon, to act the fear of a dragon, and at the same time to make a noise expressive of a dragon, is" (as Sir George Dyson has dryly noted) "a form of tautology open to serious criticism." But such sober reasoning is not likely to occur to any raptly absorbed, participating listener to Wagner's *Ring*. And if this very tautology, this extravagance of diverse and multiplied appeals, is a crude, shotgun attack on the listener's susceptibilities, it is sure to find a vulnerable spot if one exists anywhere in the target area.

For the home listener, the characteristic multiplicity of opera provides a wide choice of approaches. Listeners instinctively biased toward extravert, big, vocal music have a great advantage, particularly with the most popular standard works. Those less favorably disposed to accept the extreme conventions of this repertory, however, have many other entrées to the operatic world: sometimes through familiarity with composers known by their music in other forms; often with operas already known in part through concert-performance recordings of orchestral, aria, or ensemble-scene excerpts.

My first suggestions for a complete novice in this field are: Johann Strauss's *Die Fledermaus*, for its wealth of frank melodic, rhythmic, and coloristic appeal; Bizet's *Carmen*, often acclaimed as the perfect combination of drama, tunefulness, animation, and color; and Verdi's *Aida*, a grandscale panorama of the finest Italian operatic traditions.

The next steps are more critical, for you must decide—from these samples or your previous experience—whether to follow the bandwagon approach or to seek less welltrodden paths. If the former, the logical selections include: Verdi's *La Traviata, Rigoletto,* and *Il Trovatore;* Puccini's *La Bohème, Tosca,* and *Madama Butterfly;* the inseparably billed twins, Leoncavallo's *Pagliacci* and Mascagni's *Cavalleria rusticana;* Rossini's *Il Barbiere di Siviglia,* Donizetti's *Lucia di Lammermoor,* and Bellini's *Norma.*

The bandwagon approach might begin with either French or German warhorses no less conventionally than with Italian: Gounod's *Faust,* Massenet's *Manon,* and Offenbach's *Les Contes d'Hoffmann,* say; or Humperdinck's *Hänsel und Gretel* and Wagner's *Tannhäuser,* or—if you've already had considerable symphonic-listening experience—the latter's *Tristan und Isolde* and Richard Strauss's *Der Rosenkavalier.*

Between works like these and works of generally subtler and sometimes more complex qualities, the natural link is the multi-faceted operatic genius of Mozart. Perhaps nowhere else, in opera at least, can so many different temperaments find such extensive and solid common ground. There are Mozartean delights seemingly created with such matchless insight into your individual desires and needs that it always comes as a shock when you discover that your friends, of perhaps quite contrasting and contradictory tastes, find in the same music—but for entirely different reasons—a relish comparable to your own.

The only order of precedence I can suggest among Mozart's four great operas—*Le Nozze di Figaro*, *Don Giovanni*, *Così fan tutte*, and *Die Zauberflöte*—is that determined by shutting your eyes and seizing whichever LP set your hand lights on first. If I could have only one of them, perhaps it would be the last named, but I hope neither you nor I ever have to be backed up against so hard a wall of choice.

From Mozart you cannot really *go* anywhere—you can only turn aside. Yet once you have drunk from his fountain of eternal youth, you are surcharged with new energies that are of incomparable aid in approaching other operas, perhaps especially those whose complexities are not so invitingly accessible. This may be a good time for the broader splendors and scarcely less penetrating psychological insights of Mussorgsky's *Boris Godunov*, the heroic nobility of Beethoven's *Fidelio*, the joyous vitality of Smetana's *The Bartered Bride*, the somber yet serene eloquence of Gluck's *Orfeo*, the radiant immensities of Berlioz's *Les Troyens*, and the shadowed, ineffably poignant dream-world of Debussy's *Pelléas et Mélisande*.

For many it also may be the time when they can surrender whole heartedly to the imperious sorcery of that master magician Wagner and allow themselves to be drawn first into the sun-warmed world of *Die Meistersinger*, then into the fantastic sub- and super-human other world of *Der Ring*, and the mystic realm of *Parsifal*. For others, clinging to the less strained humanity of the Italians, there will be rewards of quite different kinds in Donizetti's lusty *Don Pasquale*, the icy magnificence of Puccini's *Turandot*, the fresh pastoral breadth and passion of Rossini's *Guglielmo Tell*, and Verdi's twin apotheoses of the comic and tragic spirits, *Falstaff* and *Otello*.

Some listeners, not primarily operatically inclined, may be willing to dwell on some of these heights for a time and then insist on pressing on to other musical realms entirely. But they will deny themselves many precious experiences if they fail to venture both farther back and forward in operatic time: in one direction to Purcell's *Dido and Æneas*, Rameau's *Hippolite et Aricie*, Monteverdi's *Orfeo*, Alessandro Scarlatti's *Il Trionfo dell' onore*, Vecchi's madrigal "opera" *L'Amfiparnasso*, and at least some examples of Carissimi's or other early operas and pastoral plays; in the other direction to Ravel's *L'Enfant et les sortilèges*, Thomson's *Four Saints in Three Acts*, Stravinsky's *The Rake's Progress*, and Berg's psychopathological but Medusa-fascinating *Wozzeck* and *Lulu*.

Just as the unflagging high spirits and graciousness of Mozart provide a meeting-place for listeners of widely diverse tastes, almost everyone can mingle happily on the great common ground of light or comic opera, *opéra comique*, and operetta. Begin as far back as Pergolesi's *La Serva padrona* and Pepusch's *Beggar's Opera*, or as recently as Gershwin's *Porgy and Bess*, Rodger's *Oklahoma!*, Porter's *Kiss Me Kate*, and Weill's *Lost in the Stars*. Sooner or later you'll reach the British, Viennese, and Parisian oases of musical-dramatic joyfulness: Sullivan's *Pinafore*, *Pirates of Penzance*, *Patience*, and *Princess Ida;* Johann Strauss's *Zigeunerbaron*, Lehar's *Zarewitsch* and *Die lustige Witwe;* Christiné's *Phi-Phi*, Lecocq's *La Fille de Mme Angot*, and Offenbach's *Orphée aux Enfers*—to name only a few.

The true specialist, of course, will never be content to stop with any basic opera list. The following added entries can serve him only as reminders of other standard or otherwise significant works: Berlioz's semi-operatic *La Damnation de Faust*, Bizet's *Les Pêcheurs de Perles*, Boïto's *Mefistofele*, Borodin's *Prince Igor*, Donizetti's *L'Elisir d'amore* and *La Fille du régiment*, Dvořák's *Rusalka*, Flotow's *Martha*, Giordano's

Andrea Chenier, Halévy's *La Juive*, Menotti's *The Consul* and *The Medium*, Meyerbeer's *Les Huguenots*, Mozart's *Die Entführung aus dem Serail* and *Idomeneo*, Nicolai's *Die lustige Wieber von Windsor*, Ponchielli's *La Gioconda*, Puccini's triptych (*Il Tabarro, Gianni Schicchi, Suor Angelica*), Saint-Saëns's *Samson et Dalila*, Spontini's *La Vestale*, Richard Strauss's *Elektra* and *Salome*, Tchaikovsky's *Eugen Onegin*, Verdi's *Un Ballo in maschera, Don Carlo, Ernani*, and *La Forza del Destino*, Wagner's *Lohengrin*, and Weber's *Der Freischütz*.

Even this list barely skims the available LP repertory (itself mushrooming at a fantastic rate) and I skip entirely the innumerable recorded operatic excerpts, scenes and arias, and overtures. Some of the orchestral excerpts will appear later, but any discussion of isolated arias falls outside the scope of these pages. Their main attraction is less their music than their singers, and hence for most listeners matters of highly personal choice and evaluation. Enjoyable and valuable as such records may be, their collector scarcely can enlarge his horizons as long as he confines himself to fragments rather than whole works, or so long as music serves as a vehicle for performer, rather than performance as a musical medium.

Yet while I am deliberately trying to keep your attention focused on music rather than its performers, the latter unquestionably contribute significantly to the strong sense of participation achieved by opera specialists. Along with the dramatic and pictorial attractions of opera, there is a special appeal exerted by its individual characters. Some listeners even identify themselves with some of the leading players, but anyway they clearly recognize and differentiate among them. This is done partly on the basis of role characteristics, as devised and developed by composer and producer, but it is also achieved independently by the personalities of the actual performers who take these roles: the visual qualities of their appearance, gestures, and expressions, if seen in the opera house, but in addition by their purely vocal individualities in recorded as well as live performances.

Perhaps the major reason why a novice listener has difficulty in following a strictly instrumental work is that he fails to identify and differentiate among its tone "characters"—though these too are strongly personalized by both the composer and the individual player. It may be harder to recognize a specific oboist's or trumpeter's style than that of a singer, yet it is done almost automatically by experienced listeners.

One thing is sure: the cultivation of this ability to follow the interplay of individual characters, whether vocal or instrumental, programmatic or thematic, enhances our sense of participation in every kind of music we hear. Through it we best understand what is going on—and why. The opportunities that opera provides for training yourself in tonal personality-recognition are perhaps most helpful among the many steppingstones that link this realm of music with others. For some listeners, opera may well be a self-sufficient world. By others, however, it can be cherished both for itself and for its wide-open gateways that lead so invitingly elsewhere.

19. Outward Drama: Ballet

I could only believe in a God that would know how to dance.
　　—NIETZSCHE: *Thus Spake Zarathustra*

THE close kinship of opera and ballet is unmistakable: in each, music not only serves as the setting for enacted events, but is in itself both expression and illumination of that dramatic action. The natural keys to listener participation, when such music is heard independently on records, are a general knowledge of the plot and the ability first to recognize the leading actors (here by their tonal characteristics alone) and then to follow the involvements and resolutions of their fates.

If you like to run a mental movie of action-images as you listen, it does not matter how accurately these correspond with actual stage productions as long as they appropriately match the ebb and flow of musical feeling. Indeed, you may need no visualization fancies at all, but be completely satisfied by the dramatic excitement aroused by purely tonal stimuli. In either case, the drama tends to counteract all but the most stubborn vocal-instrumental biases. And ballet music often has the further advantage (noted earlier, Chapters v and vi) of combining extravert and introvert appeals, as well as strongly fascinating—if on quite different levels—both novice and experienced listeners.

In particular, ballet music is a subtly persuasive tone-educator. Its rhythmic animation catches and holds fast even untrained listeners' attention, while its vivid coloring powerfully stimulates their discrimination of instrumental timbres. Small wonder, then, that it serves so effectively as a natural bridge, leading in either direction, between operatic and symphonic music, and as a rich field of specialization for listeners of widely diverse experience and tempermental predisposition.

If you are well versed in complete operas, you are already familiar with at least one segment of the ballet repertory: such bandwagon perambulators as the ballet music from Gounod's *Faust* and Verdi's *Aïda*, the Dance of the Hours from Ponchielli's *La Gioconda*, the Bacchanale from Saint-Saëns's *Samson et Dalila*, and the Dance of the Apprentices from Wagner's *Die Meistersinger*.

Yet most of these have become so hackneyed that you probably will want to press on to ballet pieces drawn from less familiar operas, or at least embodying fresher vitality: the *Danse slave* from Chabrier's *Le Roi malgré lui*, the dances from Glinka's *A Life for the Tsar*, the Handel-Beecham *Great Elopement* and *Origin of Design*, Mozart's *Idomeneo* ballet, the Persian dances from Mussorgsky's *Khovanshchina*, the Offenbach-Dorati *Helen of Troy* suite, the ballet music from Rimsky-Korsakov's *Snow Maiden* and Rossini's *Guglielmo Tell*, and Wagner's *Tannhäuser* Bacchanale.

When we turn away from operatic sources, I might make a similar distinction between classical ballets that have maintained their stage popularity largely as apt vehicles for star dancers, and those whose music retains more vital independent life. The true balletomane will have stage-production associations that lend added zest to his home listening, but others probably will find more limited, if not trivial, pleasure in the recordings of works like Adam's *Giselle*, Delibes's *Coppélia* and *Sylvia*, and Glazunov's *Seasons*, or in orchestration medleys like *Les Sylphides* and *Carnaval*, which perhaps detract more than they add (musically) to the charm of the original Chorin and Schumann piano pieces.

The mere fact that a ballet score has been arranged, however, is certainly no inherent disadvantage. Witness such happy collaborative examples as those by Handel and Beecham mentioned above. Or such sparkling works as the Boccherini-Françaix *Scuola di ballo*, Boyce-Lambert *Prospect before Us*, Gottschalk-Kay *Cakewalk*, Meyerbeer-Lambert *Patineurs*, Rossini-Respighi *Boutique fantasque*, Rossini-Britten *Matinées* and *Soirées musicales*, Scarlatti-Tommasini *Good-Humored Ladies*, Strauss-Dorati *Graduation Ball*, and Sullivan-Mackerras *Pineapple Poll*.

As a matter of fact, some well-nigh ideal ballet works actually were composed with concert rather than staged performance in mind, and may be heard with or without ballet-production connotations as you prefer. The music remains the same, though your own—or the conductor's—direction of approach may markedly shift its balance of elements. Listen, for example, to several different disc editions of Debussy's *L'Après-Midi d'un faune*, Rimsky-Korsakov's *Scheherazade*, and the Weber-Berlioz or Weber-Weingartner *Invitation to the Dance* (*Le Spectre de la rose*). Which conductors stress the ballet elements and which seem to strive for a straight concert reading?

The list of such works, in which alternative treatments are equally legitimate, can be extended to include Balakirev's *Thamar*, Bizet's *Jeux d'enfants* and Symphony in C,

Chabrier's *Suite pastorale* (*Cotillion*), Chausson's *Poème* (*Jardin des lilas*), Mozart's *Sinfonia concertante* K.364, Rimsky-Korsakov's *Capriccio Espagnole*, and Schoenberg's *Verklärte Nacht* (*Pillar of Fire*); as well as others like Beethoven's Seventh Symphony, Borodin's Second (*Bogatyri*), and Brahms's Fourth (*Choreartium*), which most of us are likely to keep on thinking of as primarily symphonic rather than ballet works.

Unlike these last, some other well-known symphonic works are essentially ballet in nature, altogether apart from the existence or absence of staged productions: incidental music like Grieg's *Peer Gynt* and Bizet's *L'Arlésienne* suites, For my own part, indeed, I find it hard to make arbitrary generic distinctions between Debussy's tennis ballet *Jeux* and his orchestral *Images*, or between Ravel's *Boléro*, *La Valse*, and *Valses nobles et sentimentales* (*Adelaïde*), and his *Rapsodie espagnole* and *Le Tombeau de Couperin*.

But of course the supreme masterpieces of theatrical dance music have been created within the great ballet tradition in the close collaboration of composer and choreographer. This is particularly true of Tchaikovsky's ballets, which exhibit a wealth of attractions unsurmised by those who get no nearer his full-length works than a few well-worn excerpts, too often played with an insensitive incomprehension of their graciousness, buoyancy, and dramatic magic. We still can get only a hint (in the so-called *Second Nutcracker Suite*) that the too familiar First barely scratches the surface of the whole work from which these are drawn. Happily, we now have substantially complete LP editions of those inexhaustible treasure-houses of delight—*Sleeping Beauty* and *Swan Lake*.

Stravinsky has fared better, though far too many listeners still lose the integrated drama of *Petrouchka* by accepting the concert suite only, or by entering only part way into the enchanted forest of *L'Oiseau de feu*. And some who follow him even into the primeval worlds of *Le Sacre du printemps* and *Les Noces* stop short of his impish metamorphoses of Pergolesi in *Pulcinella*, or his fruitful re-animation of the great classical ballet tradition in the luminous *Apollon Musa-*

gète, piquant *Baiser de la fée*, lucid yet zestful *Danses concertantes*, bustling *Jeu de cartes*, and poignantly somber *Orpheus*.

Works like these, obviously, should form the central core of any ballet-disc collection, but even they barely sketch the tropical luxuriance of species diversification so characteristic of this field. They do indicate, however, how natural it is, in this repertory, to move forward in time. It seldom is easier to penetrate the surface difficulties of contemporary music than in response to the dramatic, dynamic, and coloristic stimuli of many modern ballet works.

Indeed the "modernisms" of the lesser Russian composers are little more than spicy frostings on almost old-fashioned, fruitily melodic cakes: Glière's *Red Poppy*, Kabalevsky's *Comedians*, Khachaturian's *Masquerade* and *Gayne*, and even Shostakovich at his juvenile-delinquent sauciest in the polka from *L'Âge d'or*. The far greater Prokofiev is unfortunately less approachable in *Chout* (*Buffoon*) and *Le Pas d'acier*, or the *Scythian Suite* (not written expressly for ballet production), which ranks close to Stravinsky's *Sacre* as one of the few great monuments to the early twentieth century's brief preoccupation with realistic naturalism. Yet this last work, for all its severity to tender ears, makes up for its harshness by its electrifying atmospheric and dramatic power.

Latter-day Frenchmen and Spaniards seem to have a special affinity for brilliantly orchestrated ballet or quasi-ballet music, as is revealed in distinctively individual ways in Auric's *Les Matelots*, Chabrier's *España*, Falla's *El Amor Brujo* and *Three-Cornered Hat*, Ibert's *Divertissement* and *Escales*, Milhaud's *La Création du monde* and *Le Bœuf sur le toit*, Roussel's *Festin de l'araignée*, and Satie's *Parade*. And it's scarcely happenstance that a composer of both French and Basque ancestry should write a ballet score that is one of the most kaleidoscopic tapestries in the whole history of sound-weaving: the *Daphnis et Chloë* of Maurice Ravel.

Yet there is no real national monopoly on effective ballet and symphonic dance writing. Witness Bartók's *Miraculous Mandarin* and Dance Suite, Berner's *Triumph of Neptune*, Hindemith's *Symphonic Metamorphoses* after Weber, Kodály's

Dances from Galanta, and Lambert's *Rio Grande*. Or, from our own countrymen, Bernstein's *Age of Anxiety*, Carpenter's *Adventures in a Perambulator*, Copland's *Billy the Kid* and *Rodeo*, Gilbert's *Dance in the Place Congo*, Gould's *Interplay*, Moross's *Frankie and Johnny*, and William Schuman's *Judith*.

Moving backward in time generally is less exciting, yet it would be a lopsided ballet library that ignored Schubert's *Rosamunde* music, Beethoven's *Geschöpfe des Prometheus*, Mozart's *Petits Riens*, the popular Gluck Ballet Suite arranged by Mottl, and the more authentic and even finer *Don Juan*, or the Grétry-Mottl *Céphale et Procris* suite. And the true specialist will not stop there, still short of such gracious examples of the rococo and baroque spirit as the ballets and dance suites of Lully, Rameau, and Couperin, the masque and other incidental music by Purcell; Monteverdi's *ballo concertante*, *Tirsi e Clori*, or the best of later-day transmutations of early lute and viol music, such as Respighi's *Ancient Airs and Dances*, and Warlock's *Orchésographie*.

From the phonographic listener's point of view, at least, it is foolish to define ballet music too literally. Some of its most distinctive characteristics (apart from theatrical point and scale) appear in many orchestral, ensemble, and solo evocations of the dance spirit. From the suites by Bach, Handel, and other baroque composers, we can go on through Haydn's, Mozart's, Beethoven's, and Schubert's German-dance, contradance, and *Ländler* precursors of the waltz, to Straussian examples both of the perfected waltz itself and of its jauntier sister, the polka, and to the apotheoses of national and regional traditions in the dances and dance cycles by Bartók, Brahms, Chopin, Dvořák, Grainger, Granados, Grieg, Smetana, and many other composers.

The hardest problem in building up a ballet-disc library is knowing where to stop. The bright arterial blood of the dance pulses through the veins of all living music. But if few other specializations are as likely to burst whatever practical bonds we try to put on them, surely no other provides its collectors with more stimulating relish or easier approach-links with other, even seemingly far distant, musical realms.

20. Inward Drama: Symphonic Music

*It isn't simple at all . . . It's desperately
complicated. But at the end there's light.*
—STEINBECK: *East of Eden*

THERE are fundamental as well as surface differences between music provided with a verbal text or program and
that lacking any explicit key to what it is all about. Yet in
most large-scale works the essential dramatic kinship of
these two general types is even more striking than their
external dissimilarities. Only the novice, his mind clouded
by fuzzy notions and misconceptions, exaggerates the latter's importance.

This exaggeration often brakes his free movement from
one type to the other. Sometimes it spurs him in one direction only: just because the inward drama of so-called pure
music is popularly assumed to be harder to appreciate, he
yearns for it all the more earnestly. However laudable this
naïve attitude may be, it is dangerously likely to warp
æsthetic judgments, and many novices tend, at least unconsciously, to rank readily understandable music as inferior to that which for them is surrounded by an aura of
impressive mystery.

Such awestruck symphonic neophytes might profit by
studying the more open-minded approach of children or
their own immediate, unconsidered reactions, in which music commands response quite regardless of its generic type.
Obvious, programmatic works usually are the most sure-
fire in this respect, but it is surprising how often any of us
can be pleasurably tickled as well as impressed by music
supposedly beyond our powers of appreciation. Two of the
most significant features of the enormous current popularity
of serious recorded music are that the symphonic repertory
finds an even wider audience than opera, and that this audience certainly is *not* split into two opposed groups, one of

which listens only to ballet and symphonic poems, while the other (presumably confined to connoisseurs) concentrates on concertos and symphonies.

I have already indicated some of the linkages among various musical media and forms, but for those who may want a highly simplified approach to the symphonic repertory, let's see how the surface differences may here be effectively if crudely explained and reconciled.

(1). Strip sung arias, recitatives, and choruses from opera, and what is left provides the materials for symphonic overtures, entr' actes, and suites. Or replace singers with dancers, and you have ballets. (2). Compress an opera or ballet into one or several key episodes, and (if you remove the singers or dancers) you have symphonic poems, or (if you substitute one or several solo instruments as protagonists) you have concertos. (3). Then an absolute symphony may be considered as a concerto without a clearly defined soloist, or as a dramatic work in which the plot is expressible not in words or pictorial images, but wholly in tonal terms, in the interplay of tensions and relaxations of feeling, and in the dramatic conflicts of distinctive themes and tonalities.

Naturally, these are gross simplifications of highly complex differentiations, but they may be helpful at first, when the listener usually is bothered less by the difficulties in the music than by those in his own mind. Undue self-consciousness and timidity are perhaps the greatest handicaps to learning that before we can hope to understand the music, we must hear it speaking directly and persuasively for itself.

For younger, more adventurous, less inhibited listeners, the best approach is simply to plunge in, following their individual tastes and good-tune or other touchstones. For those who feel the need of a more systematic, graduated orientation, the most effective progression may be via opera and ballet to overtures, suites, and film music, then to symphonic poems, and finally to concertos and symphonies. But it is well to remember that normally any such line of attack is easily reversible. For many of the new phonographic audience the movement is more likely to be *from* concertos and symphonies to opera in one direction and to chamber music in another.

Opera and ballet listeners will be already familiar with a good part of the overture, incidental music, and film-score repertories. When you now approach them as independent concert works, whatever previous knowledge you may have (of either melodic materials or dramatic situations) can help you in concentrating more closely on the instruments and sound textures. The vital initial factor in symphonic understanding is a shift in attention from dramatic events on a real or imaginary stage to those taking place entirely within the orchestra.

The conciseness and clear-cut mood definitions of overtures are notably effective in arousing a high degree of listener attention and sense of participation. Begin with any of the familiar operatic examples, but for purposes of orchestral study the most rewarding probably are those by Gluck, Mozart, Berlioz, Rossini, Wagner, and Weber. Then, there being no inherent musical differences in the concert-overture form, it is easy to move directly on to compact expressions of Beethoven's most characteristic qualities in *Coriolanus*, *Egmont*, *Leonora* No. 3, and the even more dramatically powerful *Consecration of the House;* to Berlioz's *Carnaval romain* and *Le Corsaire*, and Brahms's *Academic Festival* and *Tragic* overtures.

Most incidental-music and film-score suites, less tightly integrated and involving a greater variety of moods, have special advantages for novice approach, not the least of which is their natural separation into sections that make comparatively modest demands on your attention-staying powers. I have already suggested a number of such works in the preceding chapter, and now those might be augmented, first by Mendelssohn's *Midsummer Night's Dream* music and some of the suites from or "symphonic syntheses" of Wagnerian operas; then by Britten's *Young Person's Guide* and *Peter Grimes* Sea Interludes, Copland's *Our Town* and *Quiet City* scores, Kodály's lusty *Háry János* suite, Prokofiev's *Lieutenant Kijé* suite and mighty symphonic cantata from the film *Alexander Nevsky*, Thomson's *Louisiana Story* and *The Plow that Broke the Plains*.

SYMPHONIC POEMS AND PICTURES

In the form dearest to the heart of the ultraromantics, the canvas may be either large or small, but its various elements invariably are closely integrated to give a more unified, dramatic effect. Some of the most popular examples have been mentioned earlier (Chapters v and vi); others that correspond similarly with an operatic or ballet scene or episode include: Franck's *Le Chasseur maudit*, Gershwin's *An American in Paris*, Liszt's *Les Préludes*, *Orpheus*, and *Mephisto Waltz* (orchestral version), Saint-Saëns's *Danse macabre*, and Sibelius's *Tapiola*. And you will find even stronger dramatic impacts, as well as larger symphonic scope, in Debussy's *Ibéria* and *Nocturnes*, the Mussorgsky-Ravel *Pictures at an Exhibition*, Richard Strauss's *Don Juan*, *Till Eulenspiegel* and *Tod und Verklärung*, and Tchaikovsky's *Romeo and Juliet* and *Hamlet*.

Some of the latter are epic rather than lyric tone-poetry, and the fine distinction between symphonic poem and programmatic symphony or concerto is whittled away to nothing in such tremendous tone-dramas as Berlioz's *Symphonie fantastique*, *Harold en Italie*, and *Roméo et Juliette*, Debussy's *La Mer*, Strauss's *Don Quixote* and *Ein Heldenleben*, and Tchaikovsky's *Manfred*.

CONCERTOS

Moving on to the modern type (as distinguished from the older *concerto grosso*, which I am saving for Chapter xxii), the loss of a verbal program is compensated for here by the gain of an easily identified and followed hero. Enacted in tonal terms alone, the drama no longer is provided with an explicit plot, but it obviously comprises much more than a leading actor's soliloquy delivered against a discreet musical background. The essence of the drama lies in the hero soloist's involvement in high adventures—in which the other instruments participate too, and for which the revelatory materials are themes, tonalities, and sonorities.

Many listeners find it easiest to follow both these materials and the leading tone-actors in the broadly rhetorical unambiguously expressive, ultraromantic showpieces, usually beginning with such bandwagon hits as the piano and violin concertos (mentioned in Chapter ii) by Beethoven, Brahms, Bruch, Chausson, Franck, Grieg, Lalo, Liszt, Rachmaninoff, Schumann, and Tchaikovsky. But from these it is to go on to less hackneyed works by some of these composers or others exemplifying more diversified or more subtly particularized qualities: piano concertos such as Beethoven's delightful first three, Brahm's First, Liszt's Second and *Todentanz*, Rachmaninoff's First and Fourth, Tchaikovsky's Second and Third, plus those by Delius, Dvořák, Mac-Dowell, Mendelssohn, Rimsky-Korsakov, Rubinstein, Saint-Saëns, Scriabin, Strauss (*Burleske*), and Weber (*Konzertstück*); violin concertos by Elgar, Glazunov, Paganini, and Sibelius; cello concertos by Bloch (*Schelomo*), Dvořák, and Schumann; Brahms's double and Beethoven's triple concerto; and those for clarinet by Weber and trombone by Rimsky-Korsakov.

Outside ballet music, some of the most inviting approaches to more modern composers are such concertos as those by Bartók (piano, violin, viola), Gershwin (piano), Khachaturian (piano, violin), Martinů (*Sinfonietta Giocosa* for piano), Prokofiev (piano—especially No. 3—violin), Ravel (piano), Shostakovich (piano), Stravinsky (piano *Capriccio*), Thomson (cello), and Walton (violin).

Mozart's last, larger piano concertos properly belong in this chapter, but I am holding them back for later discussion. Anyway, the Mozartian corner of this field is a world in itself, for which a guide is superfluous, once you venture into its enchanted domain.

SYMPHONIES

Here, too, the embarrassment of riches makes exorbitant demands. I have always believed in skipping the standard masterpieces, which can be heard so often in concerts, in broadcasts, and at friends' houses, to concentrate on the works we can learn by heart only, or—best—by ourselves at home. But no one, including myself, ever is willing to abide consistently by such a Spartan rule.

Few novices at least can, or perhaps should, deny themselves rapturous puppy-love affairs with Schubert's "Unfinished," Franck's D minor, Dvořák's "New World"; the other immensely popular symphonies (mentioned in Chapters ii and iii) by Beethoven, Bizet, Brahms, Mendelssohn, Prokofiev, Schubert, Sibelius, and Tchaikovsky; and such comparable favorites as Beethoven's "Pastorale," Mendelssohn's "Scotch," Mozart's K.543 and K.550, Rachmaninoff's Second, Schumann's First and Fourth, and Sibelius's Second and Fifth. Anyone who has grown to musical maturity without having such crushes certainly is to be pitied. Yet I pity even more the listener who does not eventually break loose from such blissful adolescent thralldom.

He will return, of course, to many of them, to find maturer rewards in a more adult (if surely never platonic) relationship. But meanwhile more provocative stimuli are to be found in less hackneyed works, which provide sharper insights into our favorite composers, as well as wider perspectives for their full stature.

Range, for example, more widely in the standard classical-romantic repertory: Beethoven's Second and Fourth, Borodin's Second, Brahms's Second and Third, Bruckner's "Youth" and Fourth, Dvořák's First, Second, Fourth, and early Symphony in E flat; the symphonies by Chausson and d'Indy, Glière's *Ilya Murometz*, Goldmark's "Rustic Wedding," Mahler's First and Fifth, Mendelssohn's Fifth ("Reformation"), Saint-Saëns's Third, Schumann's Second and Third ("Rhenish"), and particularly Tchaikovsky's far too seldom heard first three. Then discover how later composers have endeavored both to put new wine into old bottles and to reshape the form itself to fit new contents, in symphonies by Hanson, Harris, Hindemith, Ives, Kalinnikov, Miaskovsky, Milhaud, Nielsen, Prokofiev, Roussel, Sibelius (Third),

William Schuman, Sessions, Shostakovich, Stravinsky, and Vaughan Williams (Sixth).

Then, at last, you may be fully equipped to strike deep into the heart of works that formerly satisfied you merely by their most superficial attractions. And to grapple fairly with the profundities of Haydn's No. 102 and other "London" symphonies, Mozart's K.551 ("Jupiter") and his other last symphonies, Beethoven's Ninth, Schubert's Ninth (C major), Liszt's "Faust," and Bartók's Concerto for Orchestra. Also, if they hold grandeur rather than grandiosity for you, Bruckner's Seventh and Ninth, Mahler's Eighth and Ninth, and Sibelius's Fourth and Seventh.

So hasty a sketch can only rough in the main outlines of a symphonic disc library's potential dimensions. It scarcely even implies the incredible diversity with which composers have invested the superbly flexible forms of overture, suite, symphonic poem, concerto, and symphony. And at that I have been forced to skip many works in variation or other forms for large orchestra (some of which, however, are discussed in Chapter iv), as well as to hold back the whole baroque and rococo orchestral repertories for a later chapter.

No matter how broadly or narrowly we set our limits, it is seldom practicable to achieve the comprehensiveness we should like a symphonic library to have. And perhaps that is just as well, for multitudinous, inviting, and exciting as this realm is, there still are many others to visit, if not to conquer. Yet, for all that, it is here that the majority of phonographic listeners feel most at home. Even the others rarely if ever can fully free themselves from the symphonic realm's enchantment. The strength and soaring imagination of the many geniuses who built this world forever remain—for all of us—supreme challenges to the utmost response of which our own minds and hearts are capable.

21. Inward Drama: Music for Worship

For if such holy Song
Enwarp your fancy long
Time will run back, and fetch the age of gold.
—MILTON:
Hymn on the Morning of Christ's Nativity

MATTHEW tells us that it is more difficult for the rich to enter into the kingdom of God than for a camel to go through the eye of a needle—a pertinent warning for contemporary listeners seeking entrance into music's ageless sacred realms. The very notion of a solitary individual's sitting back at ease in his living-room to *listen* to a Victoria motet, Palestrina Mass, or Bach chorale would have been almost inconceivable to those composers and the congregations who originally shared in the performance of such devotional works.

The ideal approach, perhaps the only proper one, is the ancient one of faith—the "clamor of every soul to its God." Yet even for those of us who cannot, or will not, participate completely in this music as an act of divine worship, it still can be an active and exalted *æsthetic* experience. Fired by its radiant warmth, even we cannot remain wholly insensible to its spiritual power. Even on the lower level of merely human drama, what physical or intellectual adventures of mankind can excite and absorb us more profoundly than those of the soul?

From a spiritual point of view, the church music of recent centuries lost much of its serene purity when it added to the natural resources of voices alone those of the modern orchestra. Yet for the present-day listener, primarily versed in secular dramatic music, these very "impurities" serve as a familiar means of approach.

Oratorios, for example, are basically operas on a Biblical (or sometimes pantheistic) subject. Designed for concert rather than staged performance, they are admirably suited for home listening, where it is always easier to imagine appropriate dramatic action than in the constrained, formal atmosphere of the concert hall or church. As in opera, the verbal texts provide a master key, and the best-known classical-romantic oratorios have the further advantage of largely familiar tonal materials. Their melodic contours, harmonic idioms, and accompanying orchestral treatment generally have been absorbed in childhood, or at least are closely akin stylistically to those of well-known operatic and symphonic works.

The natural, if roundabout, approach to church music begins, then, with the great oratorios of Mendelssohn (*Elijah* and *St. Paul*) and Haydn (*The Creation* and *The Seasons*). Less familiar (and less substantial) works of the same period include those by Beethoven (*Christ on the Mount of Olives*), Rossini, Saint-Saëns, Franck, and others, but perhaps the only other one that must not be missed is the enchantingly lovely *L'Enfance du Christ* by Berlioz.

From these I suggest skipping the saccharine Victorian pieties of Stainer, Elgar, and others, and going directly to the far more rewarding modern masterpieces: Debussy's *Le Martyre de Saint-Sébastien*, Honegger's *Roi David*, Kodály's *Psalmus Hungaricus*, and Walton's *Belshazzar's Feast*, plus such outstanding contemporary oratorios on non-Biblical subjects as Honegger's *Danse des morts* and *Jeanne d'Arc*, Milhaud's *Orestie* trilogy, and Stravinsky's *Oedipus Rex* and *Perséphone*.

Most notable liturgical and quasi-liturgical works of recent centuries are (according to ecclesiastical purists) ill suited for formal church use. Yet some of them contain not only superb drama, but considerable, if not always orthodox, spirituality: Britten's *Te Deum*, Hindemith's *Apparebit repentina dies*, Holst's *Hymn of Jesus*, Kodály's *Missa Brevis* and *Te Deum*, Satie's Mass for the Poor, Stravinsky's Mass and *Symphonie de psaumes*, and the sacred services (for reformed synagogue use) by Bloch and Milhaud.

It was mainly eighteenth- and nineteenth-century composers whose liturgical works drew the fire of Pope Pius X in the *Motu proprio* of 1903. But while there may be every justification for eliminating them from actual church use, there still is a high degree of sheerly musical interest in Cherubini's Requiem, Rossini's *Stabat Mater*, Schubert's Masses, and Verdi's Requiem. There are even richer rewards in Bruckner's Masses and *Te Deum*, Fauré's serene, heart-twistingly lovely Requiem, and the overwhelming grandeurs of Haydn's Mass in Time of War (*Paukenmesse*) and Berlioz's *Messe des morts* (Requiem). Many listeners may assign equally high rank to Beethoven's *Missa Solemnis* and Brahms's *Deutsches Requiem*. And if Mozart's unfinished Requiem remains a curiously uneven work, few who know it would willingly part with it. Still less would they part with his Masses K.317 and K.427 and several shorter sacred works, or with Haydn's *Seven Last Words* and several remarkable Masses, for whose restoration many of us must be forever indebted to the efforts of the Haydn Society.

Yet until we reach back into the baroque era, we can scarcely realize the full richness of the sacred-music repertory for voices with orchestra. If there is little need to hymn anew the supreme greatness of Handel's *Messiah* or Bach's Mass in B minor and *St. Matthew Passion*, it always is well to be reminded that these are only the outstanding peaks in the Himalayan ranges that also include the former's *Israel in Egypt*, *Judas Maccabaeus*, and many other oratorios (not excluding such secular works as the incomparably delicious *Acis and Galatea*), and the latter's *St. John Passion*, *Christmas* and *Easter* oratorios, and *Magnificat*.

Most of these are known at least by repute to present-day listeners, but many oratorios and church works by their composers' contemporaries and predecessors unfortunately still command only specialist audiences: C. P. E. Bach's *Magnificat*, Buxtehude's *Magnificat*, *Missa Brevis*, and choral cantatas, Carissimi's *Jephthe* and *Jonas*, Lalande's *De profundis*, Monteverdi's *Beatus vir* and Vespers, Pergolesi's *Stabat Mater*, Purcell's *Te Deum* and anthems,

Alessandro Scarlatti's *Motetto da requiem*, Vivaldi's *Beatus vir* and *Juditha Triumphans*, and perhaps, above, all, the Passions, *Seven Words from the Cross*, and ineffably tender Christmas and Resurrection "Stories" by Schütz.

The appeal of these works is so fresh and potent that many a listener temperamentally biased toward bigness, overt drama, and symphonic sonority will hardly realize how imperceptibly he is led into a new world of experience where broad contrasts give way to relaxed, contemplative expansiveness, and where the thick richness of post-baroque coloring is replaced by the delicate interplay of purer and brighter timbre-nuances. This lesson may become even more persuasive in works that utilize still more economical tonal means to achieve a maximum of textural tautness and transparency, shot through with occasional gleaming strands of a single, intensely differentiated color. Besides the most famous choral cantatas of Bach, be sure to go on to those mainly for one or two soloists, and to the cantatas or sacred arias of Bach, Couperin, Hammerschmidt, Kriedel, Lübeck, Porpora, Purcell, Alessandro Scarlatti, Schütz, and Telemann.

For, whatever our vocal-instrumental biases, music like this irresistibly reconciles them. Listen to the same phrases tossed from players to singers to exquisitely balanced joint voicings. Then go on to hear—and join in—the chorales of Bach and other Lutheran composers, and to compare these with the Bach, Buxtehude, and other chorale-preludes, whose meditative depths of feeling owe perhaps less to the organ tones that give them sounded life than to their listeners' memory-traces of the sung melodies that are their pulsing life-blood.

The more you listen to earlier sacred music, the more forcibly you realize the rightness of the dominant part played by the human voice whenever the tone-art's essential function is the expression of religious feeling. Undoubtedly this is a basic reason why there is no truly significant literature of solely instrumental church music, at least apart from the transformed vocalism of the chorale-preludes.

In contrasting the baroque works we have surveyed so far with those of later periods, even the primarily secular and instrumental-minded listener can glimpse at least some of the reasons—technical as well as spiritual—why choral music assumes greater fluidity, expressive force, and grandeur in almost direct proportion to its elimination not only of alien, instrumental characteristics, but also of the dynamic vehemence, rigidly measured beat, and top-heavy vertical (harmonic) structure so representative of most eighteenth- and nineteenth-century composition.

When your ears and nervous systems have been thoroughly schooled in later music, it usually requires a complete un-education to readjust your sensibilities to unaccompanied vocal polyphony. It is only by listening with newly cleansed ears and souls, by learning to follow simultaneous fluid lines, by weighing the exquisite equilibrium of parts, and by feeling the cross-pulls of intricately meshed rhythms that most of us can reach a full apprehension of the infinite riches that lie in the still scarcely fathomed treasure-house of Renaissance and medieval unaccompanied Masses and motets.

This music, indeed, demands, if not a spiritual, at least an artistic rebirth, not so much for itself as for its hearers. Lucky the child who grows up in its tradition in or outside the church itself! Yet perhaps those for whom it always has been a natural part of their lives miss something of the ecstatic revelation with which it can come to the stranger, or even heretic, ready to accept it—whether for its spiritual or æsthetic values or both—on its own terms. For here there is a faith even for the faithless: a knowledge, like Whitehead's, that "our experience, dim and fragmentary as it is, yet sounds the utmost depths of reality."

Here, again, a roundabout approach may be the easiest, beginning with such fine modern unaccompanied liturgical works as Poulenc's Mass in G and Villa-Lobos's "Sebastian" Mass; such entrancing lighter music as the

Christmas-carol settings by Britten, Vaughan Williams, Holst, and others; some of the baroque composers' backward glances—Bach's and Schütz's motets, Monteverdi's *Magnificat Secundo*, Praetorius's *Singt dem Herrn*, Schein's *Die mit Tränen säen*, and so on—or even the secular madrigals of the Renaissance itself.

But no matter how indirect or long the way, eventually we must enter, with sensitized responsiveness, the incomparable tone-cathedrals that symbolize and articulate perhaps better than any stone or literary monuments the permeating religious spirit of mankind over the span of the twelfth to sixteenth centuries. Some of the eloquent composer priests we can hear there, we may have met (or later will come to meet) in lighter spirits outside the solemn shadows of the church. But nowhere else is their incredible variety of distinctive personalities so harmoniously blended —yet never entirely lost—in a common spiritual radiance. And nowhere else is the order of their æsthetic or historical precedence so unimportant.

They may be such famed giants as Victoria, Palestrina, Byrd, Lassus, Josquin, Dufay, Obrecht, and Ockeghem. They may be figures who loom smaller in our inadequate perspective on the past, like Aichinger, Anerio, Arcadelt, Clemens non Papa, Finck, Gallus, Gibbons, Gombert, Goudimel, Hassler, Ingegneri, Isaac, Morales, Morley, Nanino, and Tallis. They may stem from the Renaissance, like most of these, or from the darker, deeper past of medievalism, like Machaut, Leoninus, and Perotinus. But one and all, their Masses, motets, psalms, lamentations, and organa are sublime tributes both *ad majorem Dei gloriam*, as they were devoutly intended, and to the imperishable glory of mankind itself.

No disc library of sacred works, however limited, can deny some representation to the unison song that is the oldest and purest musical expression of worship. As exalted as the masterpieces of choral polyphony (most of which, indeed, are rooted in it), yet refined even of their traces of human artistry, plainsong has so far been served none too well by the phonograph. Too many of the recordings of Gregorian chant embody stylistic errors, and of non-Gregorian chant we have comparatively little. There is, however, a promise of more to come, and, best of all, the matchless Gregorian singing of the monks of Solesmes is soon to reappear on LP's. And it is the latter that can best bring to present-day listeners a luminous revelation of the very quintessence of all musical worship.

22. Divertimento

> . . . a casual
> Improvisation, or a settled game . . .
> Those deeds were best that gave the minute
> wings
> And heavenly music if they gave it wit.
> —YEATS: Her Triumph

DEVOTIONAL and symphonic music, opera and ballet—however varied they may be in tonal forms, media, and idioms —have an underlying dramatic kinship. They all are concerned with larger than life-size aspects of man and his fate. They all tend toward a cosmic revelation of life, both as it is and as it might be.

This may be the ideal function of all art. Certainly no other more profoundly broadens our whole experience. Yet from time immemorial men have needed playfields no less than temples and theaters. Men always have gathered together to entertain themselves in direct personality contacts and competitions, in the diverting interchange of gossip, quips, and speculation, which is the characteristic activity of informal, relaxed fellowship.

Even when serious music was devoted exclusively to the greater glory of God, there were folk and popular musics created simply and spontaneously for fun. And if later composers concentrated their most earnest efforts on new forms of dramatic expression, they also delighted in improvising for their own and their friends' amusement. Few of them ever felt it unnatural or undignified to serve as tonal artisans in preparing musical decorations for any appropriate occasion.

Such literally "occasional" music forms a special repertory, as markedly differentiated from the epic tone-dramas surveyed in the four preceding chapters as it is from the lyric poetry and miniature dramas of the "chamber" music still to be discussed. This repertory includes many dramatic and lyrical elements, but only as freed from their larger symbolic connotations and blended more or less casually into the exuberant flow of music-making for its own sake, music-making not intended to awe or enthrall its hearers, but merely to entertain them momentarily by its fascinating, kaleidoscopic play of tonal color and arabesque.

As a rule, this music calls for comparatively few performers, is non-programmatic and instrumental, and above all never takes itself too seriously. It invites, rather than demands, participation. Its primary appeal is to listeners equipped with both a well-developed sense of humor and a ready grasp of colloquial phraseology. Hence it involves peculiar problems for many of the predominantly serious, possibly humorless, but certainly uninformed music-"lovers" who approach it nowadays via recordings. Lacking a text or program key, exploiting neither the basic attraction of the human voice nor that of "bigness," usually ambiguous rather than clearly extravert or introvert in character—it runs the risk of seeming inconsequential to those anesthetic to its sportive stimulus or unable to follow its deft techniques and mercurial interplay of tonal ideas.

For many listeners, then, the most effective introduction to this repertory probably is through the familiar concerto gateway. Not the showpieces of later classical and romantic periods, of course, but the smaller-scaled, more playful vehicles that earlier classical and rococo composers devised to exercise the dexterity and ingenuity either of themselves or of fellow musicians playing before their patrons, friends, and interested amateurs.

And since the personal magnetism of Mozart is no less—
perhaps it is even more—potent here than in his "bigger"
works, his concertos are the ideal starting-point. But be
sure to hear not only the larger, last piano works (K.466
through K.595), but at least some (say K.271, K.449, and
K.450) of the earlier ones. And, whatever else you investigate in this magical realm, don't fail to make the endearing acquaintance of his concertos for other instruments:
for solo horn, bassoon, and clarinet, in particular; at least
one of the violin concertos; and the two *Sinfonie concertante*
starring string and woodwind soloists.

No other composer can welcome you quite so intimately
and cordially. Yet once your ears and mind have been
alerted by Mozart, you are far more likely to relish similarly
close, informal contact with such different, yet decidedly
stimulating, personalities as those revealed in the piano (or
harpsichord) concertos by Bach's sons and Haydn, that for
trumpet by Haydn, those for flute by C. P. E. Bach, Gluck,
and Boccherini, for viola by Karl Stamitz, and for violin
by Haydn, Nardini, and Viotti.

Once you are acclimated to the fresh, buoyant air of
this verdant realm and gradually learn to distinguish
individual instrumental voices and inflections, you will·
find it no hardship to dispense with a featured soloist.
In the light, transparently bright scoring of the smaller
orchestral works of this period, every part can be followed with ease—not only when it darts into foreground
prominence, but also as it shares in the accompaniment to
another's solo or joins (but is never submerged in) the
chorus of the whole group.

Again it is Mozart who best turns this tonal identification study into a gay game: in his Divertimentos
(K.131, 251, 287, and 334, say), Serenades (K.239, 320,
etc.), organ "sonatas" (with strings), and many early and
middle symphonies (K.183 and 201, for example). From
these the way lies invitingly open to Haydn's C major
Divertimento, another in the same key by his brother
Michael, and the small-orchestral concertos, symphonies,

and *sinfonie concertante* of C. P. E. and J. C. Bach, Boccherini, Couperin, Dittersdorf, Pergolesi, Sammartini, and Karl Stamitz.

Writing in this vein apparently appealed less to the romantics, usually yearning for intenser expressiveness, but there are a few noteworthy examples: Schubert's early symphonies, Brahms's serenades, Dvořák's Serenade, Op. 44, Wagner's *Siegfried Idyll*, Wolf's "Italian" Serenade, etc.

But later composers have rediscovered this medium for some of their most ingratiating, least pretentious revelations of personality. Sometimes the tonal ideas and idioms are novel, but it is essentially wit, playfulness, or fancifulness that distinguishes the smaller concertos and quasi-concertos by Barber (*Capricorn*), Berg (piano, violin), Bowles (two pianos), Debussy (harp *Danses*), Falla (harpsichord), Françaix (piano concertino), Glazunov (saxophone), Griffes (flute *Poem*), Hindemith (*Der Schwanendreher*, etc.), Honegger (piano concertino, *Concertino da Camera*), Ibert (flute, saxophone), Martin (winds, *Symphonie concertante*) Milhaud (violin concertino), Poulenc (two pianos), Ravel (*Introduction et Allegro*), Richard Strauss (duo-concertino), Stravinsky (piano with wind orchestra), and Webern (nine instruments).

Then there are many small-orchestral *divertissements* standing midway between symphonic and chamber music: Françaix's Serenade, Milhaud's Little "Symphonies," Prokofiev's Overture on Hebrew Themes, Stravinsky's Petites Suites, Schoenberg's *Kammersymphonie*, Varèse's *Intégrales* and *Ionisation*, and Webern's Op. 21 "Symphony." A few similar works included one or more vocal parts: Poulenc's *Bal masqué*, Schoenberg's Serenade, Stravinsky's *L'Histoire du soldat* (which calls for a narrator) and "chamber operas" *Mavra* and *Renard*, and Walton's *Façade* (which, in the original version, includes recitations).

In some of these, even in a few of the earlier classical and romantic examples, there are indications that the composers may not be wholly satisfied by their available resources, but aspire to larger symphonic and dramatic utterance. Occasionally, at least, there is an oratorical vehemence alien to the friendly argumentation and playful gusto that are the key-notes of the informal muscial *divertissement*.

Perhaps it was only in the baroque era, before the orchestra was developed into the complex apparatus we know today, that the greatest of composers could find the most economical means completely sufficient. For such men, expressiveness could lie wholly in distinctively contoured melodic and rhythmic materials themselves, presented in boldly simple dynamic, color, and sonority antitheses (loud/soft, bright/dark, rich/thin), which neither need nor tolerate the subtle nuances of inflection which spelled expression for later musicians. Played straightforwardly—with a perfectly steady pulse, unwavering "line," and evenly but always tautly woven texture—the best baroque orchestral works achieve a driving momentum that enables them to sweep through the minds (and bodies) of their hearers like a torrent of pure energy.

Music like this demands far more than passive listening. You must *feel* even more than you hear—move in and with, rather than be moved by—the great baroque concertos: Bach's for solo harpsichord (or piano), for two, three, or four keyboard instruments, one or two violins, violin and oboe; Handel's for solo oboe, harpsichord, and organ; Vivaldi's for bassoon, flute, violin, and viola d'amore. There are many of these, yet each one is distinctly individual, and none is easily exhaustible. And if you ever can tear yourself away from them, there are other scarcely less electrifying musical workouts in the oboe concertos by Albinoni, Cimarosa, Corelli, and Marcello; those for flute by Pergolesi and Telemann; and those for violin by Tartini.

You can hardly afford to pass by the somewhat better-known suites by Telemann, Rosenmüller, and of course Bach. And you certainly will not want to miss the unbounded vivacity of the Boyce "symphonies." But neither the suite nor the solo concerto form stimulated the audacious baroque sound-experimenters so keenly as the *concerto grosso*—with its cross-tensions of instrumental parts, now in opposition (a *concertino* or handful of soloists pitted against the *ripieno* or "filling-out" main ensemble of strings and harpsichord), now united in a full-voiced co-operative *tutti*.

Begin with the early Italian explorations of this form by Alessandro Scarlatti, Geminiani, Locatelli, and especially Corelli. For after such valuable strengthening exercises you should be fully conditioned to plunge boldly into the overwhelming energy-flow of the *concerto grosso* cycles of Vivaldi (one of which is so aptly named *L'Estro armonico*, or "Harmonic Inspiration"); the well-nigh infinite flood of improvisatory inventiveness in Handel's cycles, Op. 6 (strings alone) and Op. 3 (winds and strings), and the magnificent "double-choir" concertos in B flat and F; and the incomparable six "Brandenburg" Concertos by Bach.

Works like these are the supreme apotheoses not only of the baroque secular spirit, but of all music-making as a glorious game, and the zest with which genius can create and manipulate highly organized patterns of purely musical thought. They never can be fully known through your ears alone. They are to be lived with and *on*—as inexhaustible sources of life-force for the revitalization of every nerve and cell in your whole organism.

❖❖❖❖❖❖❖

23. *Chamber Music: Instrumental Ensembles*

Nothing is little to him that feels it with great sensibility.
—SAMUEL JOHNSON: *Letter to Joseph Baretti*

THE widespread illusion that most music of the divertimento type just discussed is more or less inconsequential has at least some surface plausibility—if only for those who never take the trouble to listen to it on its own terms. But I am always puzzled by two other popular myths: that chamber music is practically synonymous with string quartets, and that this is the most esoteric of all tonal realms, a sanctum sanctorum accessible only to specially qualified initiates.

To be sure, many fine works (and many more dull ones!) have been written for the familiar ensemble of two violins, viola, and cello. But this is only one of a wide variety of useful—and frequently used—small instrumental combinations, which often include winds as well as strings, in both family and mixed groupings. And some of these other media have even richer potentialities of musical expression.

The string quartet has simply been particularly lucky. It has a great theoretical advantage in the long domination of harmonic textures by four voice parts. And it has also been favored for the practical reason that when composers write for this combination they stand (or at least long stood) better chances of publication and performance than with almost any other ensemble medium. Over some two centuries this has been by far the most easily assembled group vehicle for music-making by amateurs or off-duty professionals in their own homes.

That status holds a clue to the other misconception too. What is essentially "musicians' music," composed with no thought of mass-audience appeal and normally played for the performers' private pleasure, naturally runs the risk of being considered excessively specialized, if not recondite, by outsiders. And that risk is increased whenever an untrained listener actually attends a chamber-music recital— only to hear little of the dramatic colors, dynamics, and sonorities with which his emotions are stirred by opera and ballet, symphonic and church music.

But, obviously, chamber music never was meant for concert performance before large, heterogeneous audiences. With the decline in home music-making, it might have become an archaic specialty, jealously preserved by only a few connoisseurs. The advent of the phonograph averted that fate, for recordings are ideally suited to reproduce small-ensemble performances exactly as they should be heard by a few congenial friends in their own living-rooms. Nowadays, if the ordinary listener cannot play chamber music himself, he no longer is denied access to the devotee's privilege of sharing vicariously in that glorious delight. As to every other musical realm, the way now lies open here for anyone willing to develop a truly participating response to its distinctive charms.

Listeners innately biased toward smallness and instrumental and introvert musical qualities have a considerable natural advantage, especially those who can relish the quiet pleasures of lyric enchantment and sparkling tonal conversation. For such listeners it is scarcely a step from orchestral divertimentos to similar works scored for from six to nine players: beginning with the graciously lovely Schubert Octet, but also including such varied miniature tone-panoramas as Spohr's Nonetto, Villa-Lobos's *Chôros* No. 7 (octet), septets by Beethoven, Hummel, and Saint-Saëns, and sextets by Boccherini and Copland.

As these mix strings and wind, the mainly orchestrally experienced listener should not find it hard to accept the over-all reduction in forces. And if he has developed an ability to follow individual parts closely, he may find special fascinations in such wondrously piquant scores for wind instruments alone as Mozart's Serenade K.361 (thirteen winds); octets ranging from Mozart (Serenades K.375 and 388), Haydn, and Beethoven, all the way to Stravinsky and Varèse (*Octandre*); Mozart's Divertimentos, K.213, 252, 253, and 270, Beethoven's Op. 71, and Janáček's "Youth" Sextet; or the sextet for woodwinds with piano by Poulenc, and Glinka's for piano with strings.

There may be lingering traces of quasi-orchestral sound-textures in some of the works above, but we enter wholly into a new world when the number of voices is reduced to five. To my mind, the quintet represents the chamber-music ideal: an optimum of organizable differentiation, a maximum of sonority from the minimum of means, and the happiest reconciliation of co-operative-group unity and individual-part freedom.

In evidence I cite first such transcendent examples as the beloved "Trout" Quintet by Schubert, Mozart's for clarinet, K.581, Brahms's for clarinet and for piano, and Schumann's for piano. Then, for corroboration, the magical tone-spells woven in various periods and styles for strings with flute, by Boccherini and Foote (*Night Piece*); with oboe, by Britten (*Fantasy*); with clarinet, by Weber; with horn, by Mozart (K.407); with piano, by Bloch, Dvořák, Fauré, Franck, and Shostakovich; with guitar, by Boccherini; with harp, by Bax and Malipiero. Nor should we overlook Beethoven's and Rimsky-Korsakov's Quintets for piano and winds, Stravinsky's haunting *Pastorale* for violin and woodwinds, and Prokofiev's Quintet for woodwinds and strings. And other contemporary composers delight in writing for five wind instruments alone: Hindemith, in particular, with his saucy *Kleine Kammermusik*, Op. 24, No. 2; but also Françaix, Ibert, and Milhaud, to cite only a few of the best-known.

Although we have now worked our way down to quartets, I still want to defer those (as well as larger ensembles) for strings alone. For I hope you'll first investigate what can be done with other foursomes: winds alone, in quartets by Rossini and Villa-Lobos (*Chôros* No. 4); winds with piano, by Milhaud (Sonata); the delicious flute and oboe quartets by Mozart (K.285 and 370); those for piano with strings, by Mozart (K.478 and 493), Beethoven (Op. 152), Brahms (Opp. 25, 26, and 60), Copland, and Fauré.

Familiarity with works like these provides a subtly persuasive schooling in more delicate tonal color-schemes than the chamber-music novice has ever known before. It is an invaluable means of sensitizing him to the intimacy of expressive feeling that is the only real secret of this music's sorcery. Then, when he turns at last to all-string ensembles, it is necessary only to preserve this sense of binding affinity to respond to the even subtler nuances that can be achieved within a narrower, but superbly homogeneous, tone-color spectrum.

Again it may be helpful to begin with the rich sonorities of octets, by Mendelssohn and Villa-Lobos (*Bachianas Brasileiras* No. 1); sextets, by Boccherini (Op. 24, No. 1), Brahms, Dvořák, and Schoenberg (*Verklärte Nacht*, original edition); and quintets, especially by Mozart (K.406, 516, 593, and 614) and Schubert (Op. 163), but also those by Beethoven (Op. 29), Boccherini, Brahms (Opp. 88 and 111), and Dvořák.

Then, for string quartets themselves, if you are particularly susceptible to the frankly personal expressiveness of musical romanticism, the best introductory works probably are those by Dvořák (especially Op. 96), Smetana (*From My Life*), and Tchaikovsky (Op. 11 with the famous *Andante cantabile*). If you respond to the more concentrated, understated poetic styles of later composers, you are likely to relish best the quartets by Debussy, Ravel, Berg (*Suite lyrique*), and eventually the immensely difficult, immensely rewarding Bartók quartets.

On the romantic path, the next steps lead to Borodin, Brahms, Fauré, Franck, Mendelssohn, and Schumann, perhaps plus three less familiar in this particular field: Paganini, Verdi, and Wolf ("Italian" Serenade, rewritten from a small-orchestral original). Among contemporary quartets, it may be well to acquire some fluency in the relatively conservative idioms of Bliss, Britten, Malipiero, Sibelius, Turina (*Oración del Torero*), Villa-Lobos, Walton, and others before tackling the harsher, more ambiguous works by Berg, Hindemith, Milhaud, Prokofiev, Roussel, Schoenberg, William Schuman, Shostakovich, Stravinsky, and Webern.

Yet even the most confirmed romanticist or modernist will find that this medium's distinctive fascinations were daringly explored long ago by Elizabethan and baroque pioneers: in Gibbons's fantasias, Locke's "Consorts," the "Sonettos à 4" by Alessandro Scarlatti and Tartini, and, above all, in the superb fantasias (in three and five, as well as four parts) by Purcell.

And who can deny that the quartet's golden age lies in the late eighteenth and early nineteenth centuries? Never before or since have four blended strings encompassed such eloquently communicative musical feelings as those developed so imaginatively by Boccherini and Haydn, with such heart-wrenching compassion by Mozart and Schubert, and—by Beethoven—to the utmost frontier of man's penetration of the supreme mysteries both of his own heart and of the universe itself.

The specialist never can be fully satisfied until he knows all seventy some Haydn string quartets, Mozart's twenty-three or more, Schubert's fifteen or so, and Beethoven's sixteen—plus the *Grosse Fuge* and some early works in optional quartet versions. Most of these already have been recorded or soon will be. And if few of us are likely to dedicate so enormous a record library exclusively to this repertory, no one who has come to know well even a few of its disc treasures will ever lose the poignant memory of the musical companionships they offer so freely and forge so closely.

On a generally less exalted level, the far from perfectly compatible combination of piano, violin, and cello is nevertheless the most popular of threesomes. It provides a springboard for many novices' first leaps into the whole chamber-music realm—principally by Schubert's irresistibly melodic Opp. 99 and 100 and Beethoven's dramatically poetic "Archduke," Op. 97. But along with these any list of recommended introductory trios must include some of those with piano by Haydn, Mozart, and Brahms; and, among other combinations, Mozart's K.498 with clarinet, Brahms's with clarinet and with horn, Debussy's Sonata for flute, harp, and viola, Beethoven's Serenades Op. 25 (flute and strings) and Op. 8 (strings), and the all-string Mozart Divertimento K.563.

A specialist might aspire to the complete lists of Haydn, Mozart, Beethoven, and Brahms piano trios, plus one or more of those by Dvořák, Fauré, Mendelssohn, Schumann, Tchaikovsky, Ravel, and Shostakovich; wind-string-piano examples by Haydn, Schumann, Weber, Khachaturian, and Milhaud; wind trios by Mozart (Divertimentos K. Anh. 229) and Poulenc; string trios by Boccherini and Schoenberg.

Yet few of these works are as eminently satisfactory as many baroque and rococo augmentations of the divertimento repertory in the form of trio-sonatas for various pairings of winds and strings with *continuo* (i.e., figured-bass part, usually "realized" on the harpsichord, sometimes with cello reinforcement). These boast more homogeneous, yet also more piquant sonority blends than ever are possible when the assertive piano is included. And they provide not only entirely new glimpses of the multi-faceted genius of Bach, Handel, and Purcell, but an ideal means either of first making or of warmly deepening our acquaintance with Telemann, Rameau, Lœillet, and C. P. E. and W. F. Bach.

Once known, it becomes obvious that the realms of the trio-sonata and the string quartet—indeed, the whole diversified sphere of chamber music—are remote and sacrosanct only in the jealously warped minds of a few self-appointed high priests. Freed from this fanatical delusion, we can wholeheartedly echo Mann's assertion that "there is no arrogance in the world greater than that of dividing the children of our Father into initiate and uninitiate and teaching double words." These so-called innermost circles generously welcome everyone convinced that "infinite riches" can exist "in a little room," everyone willing to forgo coarser dramatic excitements to share in the direct, intimate communication among a composer, a few players, and a truly participating listener—everyone, indeed, for whom this music can be

> *heard so deeply*
> *That it is not heard at all, but you are the music*
> *While the music lasts.*

24. Chamber Music: Duos and Solos

> And even things without life giving sound,
> whether pipe or harp, except they give a distinc-
> tion in the sounds, how shall it be known what is
> piped or harped?
> There are, it may be, so many kinds of voices in
> the world, and none of them is without significa-
> tion.
> —I CORINTHIANS, xiv, 7, 10

AN ENSEMBLE, strictly speaking, can be formed by only two players, but in musical—as well as married—couples, conflicts are as often accentuated as resolved. A working equilibrium can be achieved, but usually precariously and for relatively short intervals: it is seldom that the personalities involved can be merged in a distinctive, composite identity. And with a single player, music of course becomes a wholly individual expression, transmitting the composer's ideas with a fidelity or distortion determined by the soloist's skill and insight, but always as colored by his unfettered egoism.

What this means for the listener is that the appeal of most works in the extensive duo literature, and in the enormous ones for piano and other solo instruments, depends predominantly on their performances. Hence, as a rule, the intensity with which these repertories are enjoyed is roughly proportional to the listener's interest in the specific instruments and players concerned. Few record-buyers are likely to specialize here unless they play one of these instruments themselves (or once cherished the dream of doing so) or fervently admire at least some of its virtuoso exponents.

In any case, this vast, sprawling territory is one that stubbornly resists any simplified over-all description and organization. What it is likely to mean to you, and to what extent it should be represented in your record library, are such peculiarly personal problems that I do not dare propose even the vaguest of solutions. The best that I can do here is to conduct a kind of swift, aerial survey of this chaotic realm, spotlighting the features that seem outstanding to me, with no expectation that they will appear similarly scaled in the perspective of your own tastes and experience.

The glowing terms I devoted to baroque and rococo trio-sonatas (in the last chapter) are equally applicable to the duo-sonatas of the same periods—not only to those for violin or cello with harpsichord (or, less happily, piano) by Bach and Handel, Corelli, Galliard, Geminiani, Tartini, Telemann, Vivaldi, and others, but also to the less frequently heard, but even more delectable works with flute (or recorder) or oboe, again by Bach and Handel especially, but also by Lœillet, Marcello, and Telemann.

Apart from Beethoven's and Haydn's flute sonatas and from characteristically romantic clarinet works by Weber, Mendelssohn and Brahms, later wind-and-piano literature is dominated by modern composers: particularly by Hindemith, with sonatas for trumpet, trombone, bassoon, clarinet, and flute, although several others have written for the last two—most notably, perhaps, Berg (4 Pieces) and Debussy (*Rhapsodie*) for clarinet, and Martinů for flute.

There is a large repertory of modern sonatas or other large-scale works for violin or cello with piano, in which those by Bartók, Debussy, Ravel, and Stravinsky probably are outstanding, although the long list of other contributors runs from Barber to Villa-Lobos. But first in general public favor are the romantic and classical examples— led by Franck's Violin Sonata, the three by Brahms, and Beethoven's "Spring" and "Kreutzer." Yet there are eight other violin sonatas by Beethoven, a Mozartian treasury of some thirty, several by Schubert, and two very attractive examples by Fauré. All of these men (except Mozart, who did write one for cello and bassoon) also composed firstrate sonatas for cello and piano. And for the specialist there are additional contributions to either or both sonata repertories by Boccherini, Chopin, Dvořák, Grieg, Lalo, Mendelssohn, Rachmaninoff, Saint-Saëns, Schumann, and Richard Strauss; plus a few for two unaccompanied string instruments, by Bartók, Martinů, and (most notably) Mozart (duos, K.423 and 424).

Then, too, there are those one-time delights of amateurs, currently riding the crest of a concert-popularity wave: duos played on one or two pianos, for which the original (as distinct from a widely borrowed and arranged) literature of large-scale works ranges from J. C. Bach, Mozart, and Schubert through Arensky, Bizet, Chabrier Rachmaninoff, and Schumann to Debussy, Ravel, Satie, Bartók, and Stravinsky.

Large-scale works for an entirely unaccompanied string instrument are such technical *tours de force* that only string (or Bach) specialists are likely to relish fully the miracles achieved in Bach's six violin sonatas (partitas) and six cello suites. And perhaps only students of the instruments themselves will augment these by recordings of the Paganini Caprices (in their original form), Bartók's Violin Sonata, and that for cello by Kodály.

The greatest proportion of solo music naturally is designed or the supremely versatile keyboard instruments —organ, harpsichord, and, above all, piano. For on these only ten fingers can manipulate multiple "voice" parts and command such wide ranges of dynamic, color, and sonority resources that the expressive possibilities become almost as multitudinous as those of the orchestra.

The basic organ and harpsichord literatures are rooted firmly in the baroque and immediately adjacent eras. In later organ music there is surprisingly little to interest non-specialists, except perhaps the Brahms chorale-preludes, Franck chorales, and Mendelssohn sonatas; possibly plus Widor's or other Frenchmen's "symphonies," and an occasional modern work by, say, Hindemith, Messiaen, or Schoenberg.

More regrettably, to my mind, it may be only the historical specialist who now plunges deeply into the rapidly

growing phonographic repertory (much of it performed
on "baroque-styled" or actual baroque organs) of the masterpieces by Buxtehude, Byrd, Frescobaldi, Purcell, and
Sweelinck, and those of such legendary giants as Cabezón,
Froberger, Hammerschmidt, Pachelbel, Praetorius, Scheidt,
Titelouze, Walther, and Willaert. For even the general
listener might well find rewards there quite comparable
to those he now enjoys (if he has investigated organ music
at all) in the mighty Passacaglia, toccatas and fugues, and
preludes and fugues by Bach—and in the more intimate,
endearingly lyrical charms that await him in the same
master's chorale-preludes, Pastorale, and "trio"-sonatas.

A non-specialist also is most likely to enter the domains
of the harpsichord through their broad Bachian gateway—
whose cornerstones are the magnificent "Goldberg" Variations and that incomparable "Musicians' Bible," the
Well-Tempered Clavier, but which also includes within its
span the sturdy partitas, French and English suites, and a
treasure-chest of smaller jewels. And surely he will be led
farther into the enchanted sonatina garden where Domenico
Scarlatti's imagination flowers so phenomenally. Once
spellbound there, he will scarcely need a specialist's urging
to go on to the miniature tone-poems and expansive suites
by Couperin, Rameau, Handel, and Purcell—perhaps still
farther to those of Böhm, Daquin, Kuhnau, Pasquini,
Soler, Telemann, and many others.

Many of the best-known harpsichord works often are
performed in piano versions—usually, but not invariably,
to their disadvantage. And some of the earlier Haydn and
Mozart piano sonatas and variations are as well or better
suited to the harpsichord. Even the latter's "big" works
(Fantasia and Sonata, K.475 and 457, Fantasia and Fugue,
K.394, and Sonata, K.570, for example) sometimes seem
more appropriately colored by the distinctive tone qualities
of authentic or reconstructed early spinet-pianos than by
those of the modern concert grand. But of course the full
resources of the developed instrument are demanded by
Beethoven, especially in the mighty "Diabelli" Variations

and the towering last four of his monumental series of thirty-two piano sonatas.

Later composers have never surpassed these works in dramatic eloquence, notably as they have expanded the pianistic color spectrum and enriched the keyboard's potentialities for both lyric and percussive expressiveness. The impressionists undoubtedly exert the most potent sorceries: Debussy in his *Images, Préludes,* études, and many smaller pieces; Ravel in his *Miroirs, Gaspard de la Nuit,* Sonatine, etc. But there are many varied attractions in the piano works of Bartók, Milhaud, Poulenc, Prokofiev, Satie, and Stravinsky; singular experimentation in those by Berg, Cage, Cowell, Ives, Křenek, and Schoenberg; and something for specialized neo-romantic or eclectic tastes in the sonatas or other large piano works or cycles by Barber, Bloch, Griffes, Hindemith, Kabalevsky, Rachmininoff, Scriabin, Sessions, Shostakovich, and Villa-Lobos.

Yet pianists themselves—professional, amateur, or frustrated—almost invariably cherish the romanticists as their first and usually most enduring loves. Some may concentrate on the works of the earlier men: the meandering but prodigally rich sonatas and jewel-like impromptus and *Moments musicaux* of Schubert, or the flamboyant, prophetic fantasy of Liszt's Sonata, *Années de pèlerinage,* and études. Others may specialize in the variegated works of Albéniz, Chabrier, Fauré, Franck, or Mendelssohn; and still others in the dusky, dense shadow-world of Brahms. But almost without exception they unite in paying homage to the instrument's supreme spokesmen, Chopin and Schumann.

Perhaps the non-pianistic, non-romantically minded listener never can share fully in this rapt worship. Certainly he must think it exaggerated as long as he knows—as a non-player—only such hackneyed examples as Chopin's impromptus, nocturnes, polonaises, and waltzes; or Schumann's *Carnaval, Fantasiestücke,* and *Kinderscenen;* or even their sonatas, which are hardly distinctively characteristic of either man. To soar on the boldest sweeps of these unmatched keyboard-poets' inspiration, you must turn responsively to Chopin's Fantaisie and the best of his études, mazurkas, scherzos, and ballades—and to Schumann's Fantasie, *Humoreske*, and *Kreisleriana*.

We have glanced here, obviously, at only a small fraction of the solo piano literature, and at little more of the literatures for other instruments of various kinds, solo or paired. And if this represents only partially the enormous recorded repertory, that in turn is but a small part of the inconceivable quantities of duo and solo instrumental works which have been composed and probably relished by someone (if only the composer!) in public or private. Much of this music is ephemeral or inconsequential at best, but few record collections fail, by intent or accident, to find some space for trivialities, especially when dignified by "celebrity" performances. The extent to which they absorb your own phonographic attention is your affair and no one else's—one that rarely involves any strictly æsthetic considerations. But those who righteously disdain the trivialities need to guard themselves with special care against overlooking the precious blossoms that also flower in this weed-overrun garden.

25. Chamber Music: Songs and Madrigals

> *There is not any Musicke of Instruments whatsoever, comparable to that which is made of the voyces of Men, where the voyces are good, and the same well sorted and ordered.*
> —BYRD: *Reasons . . . to perswade every one to learne to sing* (1588)

THE SINGULAR force with which the human voice penetrates every listener, establishing immediate personality affinities or antagonisms, is a formidably double-edged weapon. It can immeasurably intensify—or insidiously neutralize—

almost any vocal composition's purely musical and verbal effectiveness. In the intimate relationship of all chamber-music experience, our instinctive reactions to songs and madrigals not only are especially vigorous, but also depend even more vitally than those to instrumental works on characteristics of individual performance.

At best, then, magnetic interpretations provide a royal entrée to this realm, even to works that otherwise might seem forbiddingly difficult. Unfortunately, however, the human voice, most sensitive and expressive of all musical instruments, is the hardest to maintain under continuous precise control. Often a superbly thrilling voice is wielded by an immature artist, while a singer of outstanding musicianship may have to work with impaired or inferior vocal faculties. The miraculously perfect marriages of voice and artistry occur rarely, and for many of them we must search far back through phonographic history, even into the pre-1926 acoustical era.

Yet if the LP repertory still has comparatively few authentic song treasures, it is rapidly growing in quantity and at least gradually in quality. The matchless older performances are steadily being transferred from early and late 78's. And young listeners eventually may have the privilege of sharing the raptures of specialist collectors over all the vocal and interpretative miracles achieved by such memorable artists as Frijsh, Gerhardt, Houston, Lehmann, Noréna, Onégin, Schumann, Supervia, Teyte, and other women; Chaliapin, Hayes, Hüsch, Kipnis, McCormack, Meili, Panzéra, Schiøtz, Schlusnus, and Tauber, among the men; and ensembles like the English Singers, John Goss's London Singers, and the Cambridge University Madrigal Society.

Even the strongest personal magnetism and most illuminating interpretative radiance are, of course, not omnipotent. Listeners innately biased against vocalism, smaller forms, and introvert qualities will probably remain insensible to the special enchantments of lieder. The art-song realm is no more exclusive a musical sanctum sanctorum than that of the string quartet, but it, too, scarcely tolerates the idly curious visitor or one impatiently insistent on obvious, coarse-grained, dramatic excitement. Unless you already possess (by instinct or self-training) a warm sense of intimate kinship with the quiet beauties of this inner world, it also demands readjustments of listener attitude and often an indirect, step-by-step approach.

Of two inviting, if roundabout pathways, the natural one for listeners mainly experienced in dramatic music is that of large-scale works for voice with full orchestra. For these are barely distinguishable from many operatic and cantata arias, and they are closely related to symphonic slow movements in which an instrumental soloist sings against a rich orchestral background.

It is surely unnecessary to stress that I am *not* recommending the ubiquitous, popularized treatments of true lieder, in which an original piano part is disarranged and inflated, almost invariably violating the whole spirit as well as the characteristic texture of the music! Such sterile, sometimes monstrous hybrids cannot be used even by gullible or dull novices without harmful results.

Anyhow, there is no need for these dubious substitutes for the authentic blendings of vocal and orchestral attractions in innumerable pertinent operatic and cantata excerpts, and many individual works ranging from the evocative Berlioz *Nuits d'été* and Brahms "Alto" Rhapsody, to Berg's *Der Wein*, Britten's *Les Illuminations*, Schoenberg's *Erwartung*, Toch's *Chinese Flute*, and Villa-Lobos's *Serestas;* but including, above all, the bitter-sweet folksong metamorphoses of Canteloube's *Songs of the Auvergne*, the enchanted exoticism of Ravel's *Shéhérazade* cycle, and the purest essence of Mahler's tortured genius in his *Kindertotenlieder, Lieder eines fahrenden Gesellen,* and Rückert and *Des Knaben Wunderhorn* settings.

Some of the small orchestral works that include vocal parts (see Chapter xxii) also might be useful introductory material. A few uncommonly fine modern song-cycles call for chamber-ensemble accompaniments: Britten's *Ser-*

enade, Vaughan Williams's *On Wenlock Edge*, Warlock's *The Curlew*, and others. And occasional lieder (by Brahms, Schubert, Spohr, and others) include a string or wind obbligato part that notably enhances the appeal of these songs for predominantly instrumental-minded listeners.

The other main pathway is particularly suitable for novices grounded in "popular" song-repertories or who retain at least a subconscious craving for easy tunefulness and ballade-like verses. The songs of the best Broadway tunesmiths (Gershwin in particular), Negro spirituals and sea shanties that have not been overarranged, and simple traditional airs of various nationalities all can be used as steppingstones here. But the folksong approach by itself is not likely to lead you far until you develop a relish for settings that exhibit characteristic art-song subtlety of craftsmanship, comparable artistry of performance (as in the exquisite British examples by Kathleen Ferrier), and for a close following of the original as well as the translated texts.

Then, for more adventurous listeners, or those already fascinated by older music, there are specialized historical byways—richly rewarding for their own sake, whether or not they help in leading to the later ages of classical, romantic, and modern song. If you have an affinity for the baroque spirit, for example, you certainly should delve as deeply as the disc catalogues permit into the broadspun melodiousness of songs by Caccini, Carissimi, Frescobaldi, Monteverdi, Alessandro Scarlatti, and other Italians; by Couperin and Rameau among the Frenchmen; and by England's supreme songster, Purcell.

Plunging still farther back, you will find that the freshest, tenderest evocations of springtime and chivalrous love were created by the troubadours, trouvères, and *Minnesänger;* that the fabulous Dufay and Josquin delighted in writing secular tone-lyrics as well as grand motets and Masses; and that an international school of lutenists achieved melodic and accompaniment felicities, "framed to the life of the words," which often anticipated and never have been surpassed by either the musical or poetical gifts of later men.

These lute songs of Besard, Milan, Mudarra, Willaert, and an Elizabethan diadem crowned by Dowland, provide an ideal introduction to that most air-borne of all musical media—the madrigal. I have already tried to give (in Chapter x) some notion of the very special delights that are to be found in vocal chamber music, and perhaps need only remind you here that this incomparable treasury contains not only the brightest tone-jewels of Elizabethan England, but those of many sixteenth-century Continental composers—from such versatile giants as Monteverdi and Palestrina to so extraordinary a specialist as Gesualdo.

By comparison, at least, later secular part-song literature is scanty and inconsequential, though some listeners may relish the ribald vivacity of English Restoration "catches and glees"; the somewhat girlish sentiment of Schubert's, Brahms's, and other romantics' pieces for women's or mixed voices (usually with accompaniment); or occasional contemporary works, like the charming *Petites Voix* of Poulenc. In general, the most vital vocal inspiration of later composers has been channeled into sacred and dramatic forms when it has not been concentrated in the art-song for solo voice with piano accompaniment (or, at best, collaboration), to which the German contributions have been so dominant that the whole literature commonly is known nowadays as lieder.

The roots of the true (German) lied reach far down into the past, but the period of its full flowering barely overspreads the romantic era. There are lovely *Geistliche Lieder* by Bach and some pleasant but uncharacteristic airs by Haydn, Mozart, and the young Beethoven. But probably the first really significant work is Beethoven's *An die ferne Geliebte* cycle. And then came the bursting harvest of Schubert's incredibly fecund lyricism.

It is a poor lieder disc library that finds room only for some of the little *Ständchen* and *Ave Maria* melodies by which Schubert long has been most popularly known. His supreme genius must be sought in the superb *Schöne Müllerin* and *Winterreise* cycles. And its phenomenal extent and diversity become fully apparent only as you go on through the *Schwanengesang* collection and an almost endless list of familiar and unfamiliar individual titles.

There is much of the same sweetness, tenderness, and grace in the rich song-repertories of Franz, Mendelssohn, Schumann, and Brahms, though the non-specialist perhaps may find comparable greatness only in Schumann's *Dichterliebe* and *Frauenliebe* cycles, or the *Ernste Gesänge* and Op. 91 songs (with viola) by Brahms. The songs of Richard Strauss, too, though they contain some purer tone-poetry than his more famous orchestral and operatic works, probably appeal mainly to listeners of ultraromantic disposition. But new dimensions of lyric expression are revealed in Wolf's settings of Goethe, Mörike, and Spanish and Italian songbook texts. Certainly their poetic insights and perfect verbal-musical fusions matchlessly embody the ideals of the whole lieder tradition.

There are other Germanic byways that invite at least the specialist's exploration: Loewe's ballads; the less generally known songs of Cornelius, Jensen, Spohr, et al.; perhaps some of those by Liszt; certainly the five "Wesendonck" songs by Wagner. And it is interesting to trace the traditional forces still working beneath the surface of modern idioms in Hindemith's *Marienleben* cycle and the songs of Berg and Webern.

Most listeners, however, will find it more congenial to follow the clearer gleam of lyric romanticism in the shifting coloring it assumes in passing through other nationalistic lenses: in Chopin's Polish songs; those of the Czech Dvořák, Norwegian Grieg (especially his *Haugtussa* cycle), Finnish Sibelius, and Russian Tchaikovsky and Rachmaninoff. And many will want to pursue its further transformations in the neo-romantic and eclectic song-styles of Falla and Granados in Spain, Ives and perhaps some others in America, but particularly Britten, Vaughan Williams, Warlock, and others in England.

Yet outside the magic realm of predominantly German lieder and a few garden-oases elsewhere, there are two worlds in which the song has been more independently brought to perhaps even more distinctive flowering. One is a national domain with traditions as old and rich as those of lieder themselves. The other is an isolated, almost primitive frontier camp, established single-handed by an eccentric, unparalleled individual genius.

Without belittling the priceless heritage of German and Germanically influenced composers, I regret that their deserved fame tends to dazzle many American listeners into neglecting, if not ignoring the less effectively publicized legacies of the French art-song masters. Perhaps most of the nineteenth-century men (like Bizet, Chabrier, Chausson, Franck, Hahn, et al.) merely stamp the familiar currency of romanticism with Gallic rather than Teutonic designs. But the resources of impressionism—allied to impeccable literary and musical insight, and exploited by craftsmanship of incomparable refinement—create entirely new worlds of artistic experience in Debussy's settings of Verlaine, Baudelaire, and other poets; in Ravel's *Histoires naturelles* and other songs; in the precious handful of lyric masterpieces by Duparc and in the many by Fauré. And the chanson tradition, far better than that of the lied, continues to fire the imaginations of more recent composers, from Satie to Aubert and Sauguet, but perhaps most notably in the jeweled miniatures of Poulenc.

In Mussorgsky, present-day listeners can find even more "modern" naturalism and power: what only can be likened to a Dostoievskian voicing of humanity's normally most inarticulate feelings. His *Songs and Dances of Death*, *Sunless* and *Nursery* cycles, and many individual songs are perhaps as much psychological as musical documents. Yet they hold revelatory implications of the illimitable depths of the human soul undreamed of by the greatest of orthodox composers and indeed still to be fully plumbed by future generations of even mightier musicians, whose coming is both prophesied and prepared by this most arresting—and disturbing—of all tonal pioneers.

Collectors of solo and part songs probably always will remain a small minority group among record-buyers. No other type of phonographic specialist is obliged to devote more time and effort to building up even a small library of discs in which performance values are maintained as scrupulously as those of the musical content itself. Yet few others ever are more strongly convinced that their rewards are richly commensurate with their labors. And perhaps no other specialized repertory affords keener enticements to truly participating listening and deeper satisfactions in it.

For here even the most amateurish singer or player can have some direct experience of music-making for his own pleasure and enlightenment. Here even those who cannot (or will not) sing or play at all still have the invaluable key of poetic texts, and in addition a more closely intimate sense of imaginative identification with actual interpreters than ever is possible elsewhere. More graciously than any other music, the Song reveals its innermost meaning to every warmly responsive ear and mind, while always "preserving the sweetness of proportion and expressing itself beyond expression."

26. The Good Companions

Nobody can know what the ultimate things are. We must, therefore, take them as we experience them. And if such experience helps to make your life healthier, more beautiful, more complete, and more satisfactory to yourself and to those you love, you may safely say: "This was the grace of God."

—JUNG: *Psychology and Religion*

ANY partitioning of music's one world can be justified only as a temporary expedient. I hope that my own arbitrary divisions have been useful for our analytical survey purposes, but I hope still more that no reader accepts them as anything more than a pragmatic convenience. In the preceding eight chapters I have tried to outline the principal areas of disc-collectors' specialized interests, but many individuals are likely to find that broader or narrower boundaries better accommodate their own tastes. In any case, it is almost impossible for you to cover exhaustively even the most limited field, or—as your perceptive scope widens—to restrict your listening exclusively to any one (or two or three) of even the largest special repertories.

Some of you may prefer to plan your record-buying programs entirely differently: concentrating on the works of a favorite composer, school, or period, regardless of specific forms and performance-media; or perhaps following one or several favorite recording musicians as they range through more or less catholic repertories of solo and ensemble performances, or, if conductors, throughout operatic, ballet, symphonic, and choral music.

Yet no matter what general program or particular works you choose, no matter how systematically or haphazardly your record library develops, no matter whose advice you accept or reject, the prime shaping force always is your own personality. Your library documents your conscious and subconscious selves, revealing the evolution of your

tastes in the past and their present status, and prophesy-
ing their potential future growth. Its worth lies neither
in its comprehensiveness nor in its quality, but wholly
in its vitality.

Is your library quick—or dead? Do its contents ornament your living-room or play an integral, invigorating
role in your life? Have you assembled a museum of carefully preserved musical artifacts or a host of Good Companions with whom you can participate in far fuller,
richer experiences than any you ever find in everyday,
too often uneasy and insecure, human relationships?

What I have endeavored to put into this little book
is far less important than whatever you have been able to
get out of it, particularly in discovering new musical
friendships and ripening old ones. Whether you agree or
disagree with my frankly personal notions worries me less
than whether any of these have succeeded in firing your
own thinking. Much as you may relish some of the works
I have urged you to hear, I have not the least expectation
that you will share all my enthusiasms, or that you will not
find comparable delights in many others I may have paid
merely lip service or ignored entirely.

What I have worked hardest to accomplish is to convince you (somehow, anyhow!) that æsthetic values always
are affected by the climate of the times and the environment, that they are continuously subject to the dynamic
influences of both individual and massed listeners' reactions. If I have not succeeded in anything else, I should
be more than satisfied to have lightened the stultifying
dead weight of inferiority complex which burdens so many
novices; to have persuaded you that your personal musical
growth proceeds best with, rather than against, the grain
of your own temperament; and to have encouraged you
to enrich your experience in accord with your own basic
needs, while always remembering that these needs may
change from time to time and never are necessarily iden-
tical with those of other listeners.

In my sketchy surveys it has been impossible to avoid omitting many composers and works. But, as I look back now, none of these oversights (or even any idiosyncrasy of my selection and arrangement) seems so regrettable as my failure to stress dissimilarities as strongly as I have similarities. In any book of this kind, intent on reaching listeners of incalculably diverse backgrounds and inclination, I suppose that it is inevitable for the author to concentrate primarily on the characteristic attractions of all kinds of music and on stressing kinships that best lead the admirers of any one type to the others they are most likely to find enjoyable. The great disadvantage of this method is that some listeners, particularly those lacking confidence in their own judgments, may be shocked or discouraged when they discover that certain works they had every expectation of enjoying leave them lukewarm or cold.

So, for the benefit of any reader who has been disturbed or puzzled by his own neutral or negative reactions to some supposedly great music, even a belated consideration of this all-too-common problem may be helpful.

In any familiar repertory the differences in individuality among composers of the same period, or even among various works by the same composer, usually are obvious. But when a novice first ventures into unfamiliar realms, everything tends to sound much alike to him. You may never confuse a work by Wagner with one by Brahms, yet you are likely to be less certain in distinguishing among many of those by Haydn, Mozart, and the early Beethoven, and you may have great difficulty in recognizing the distinctive traits of most baroque and Renaissance (or ultramodern) composers, except as they are generally typical of a period's over-all stylistic character.

But it is only in the night that all cats are gray! It is only to the inexperienced that individual composers of any era fail to reveal their varied, always unique personalities. The best analogy to illustrate this point is a suburban community. To an outsider this seems to contain people all much of the same kind, typifying more or less common social standards. But to its own inhabitants and to everyone who comes to know them well, it is made up of markedly contrasted individuals, each with his own practice and philosophy of life, each with his own quirks, mannerisms, and gestures—which strike different observers in entirely different ways, as attractive or otherwise.

Beneath the general similarities of men or art in any period or locale lie the infinite varieties of individualism. And in close acquaintance it always is the individual traits that determine whether our relationships will be congenial, neutral, or antagonistic.

In the present surveys or your own explorations of the world of music, you cannot expect that, merely because someone else has found certain composers worthy of respect or admiration, you *must* share the same feelings. You may indeed "love" one or several (and not necessarily those of the greatest stature), probably "like" many others, and almost certainly dislike still others with varying degrees of intensity. For even among composers of the same school there was lively competition and conflict even in their own day. In recent centuries, at least, many artists have striven desperately to appear as much *unlike* their colleague rivals as possible. But from its earliest times music, like any other human activity, has been a medium of self-expression, and the more clearly a distinctive personality is revealed, the stronger reactions it provokes in every other personality with which it comes in contact.

So no listener, novice or experienced, need be disconcerted by his own temperamental reactions, by finding endearing affinities among lesser composers, or feeling coolly reserved—or even violently repelled—in the company of generally acclaimed masters. As in social life, our first reactions are more or less unpredictable and may be either reversed or reinforced in the course of time and closer acquaintance. Only the unmannered proclaim their private preferences, only ignoramuses assume that their preferences have the same validity for others as for themselves, and only the mean-spirited belittle any artist merely for failing to please *them*.

True discrimination of course implies an ability to distinguish great from mediocre music, but it never ensures your responding with equal warmth to every example of the former, or rejecting with equal distaste every example of the latter. We all have our blind spots, and while respect can be taught or learned, love and hate usually spring from instinctive impulses over which we can exert little conscious control.

In our personal choice of cherished companions, as in every other aspect of our musical behavior, we shall always find astonishing parallels in real life. And through them we finally can realize that artistic experience is no more—if certainly no less—mysterious than any other human activity, that here too all of us, listeners and composers alike, are creatures of infinite contradictions.

Indeed, it is this complexity, so fundamentally characteristic of our natures, that makes them so inexhaustibly interesting both to ourselves and to others. I have tried in these pages to show how significantly our musical tastes and growth are influenced by our relative responsiveness to extravert and introvert qualities, bigness and smallness, instruments and voices, drama and contemplation, epic and lyric, familiarity and unfamiliarity, comprehensiveness and specialization—all of which are never entirely either-or attractions, but complementary magnetic poles. Between each pair of dynamic stresses we can maintain an effective equilibrium only by a perpetual process of balance readjustments. Yet for most of us a state of perfect equipoise is more likely to be an ideal than an immediately practicable attainment. It is much more fun, especially in our youth, to swing vigorously to the widest extremes we are capable of reaching!

To educate ourselves in the understanding of the finest music is an admirable goal. To get the maximum listening enjoyment is a natural desire. And even these extremes are not always contradictory, irreconcilable, or unattainable.

But the first step is to remember that "understanding," "finest," and "enjoyment" all may be defined variously by different individuals, or even by the same individual at different times or stages of development.

The vital consideration for each of us is, I firmly believe, a willingness to act on—as well as accept in theory—the principle that there are all kinds of music for all kinds of purposes and all kinds of listeners, and that no individual can be permanently identified, even by himself, as any one kind of listener, utilizing any music for a single purpose. We must find our own Good Companions as befits each occasion and each of our selves.

For centuries composers, great and minor, have been making what one of them aptly described as "Musicke to content every humour, either melancholy, merry, or mixt of both." And today that incalculably rich and varied accumulation becomes increasingly accessible in our homes, on records, to choose from as and when we want. But with each act of choice, listening, and reconsideration, our experience deepens and expands. We never are quite the same again, nor can any musical work itself remain wholly unchanged for us.

That wise and great Elizabethan, William Byrd, whom I quote above, provided the best advice I know for every listener to music on records, when back in 1611 he reminded "all true lovers of Musicke" that—

a song that is well and artifically made cannot be well perceived nor understood at the first hearing, but the oftner you shall heare it, the better cause for liking you will discover: and commonly that Song is best esteemed with which our eares are most acquainted.

The infinite possibilities of repetition, of detailed study, of finding just the right mood and moment for the right experience, of transforming alien strangers into Good Companions who freely offer us entertainment, enlightenment, and eloquence limited only by our own capacities for absorbing them into our lives—these are the supreme gifts of the phonograph. And in truly Good Listening we can find wide gateways not only to the many mansions in the whole world of music, but also to the no less wondrous hidden inner world of our own personalities.

Index-Discography

Preliminary Notes

IN SOME utopian future it may be possible to produce a book on music with a magic back-cover pocket containing an economy-sized actual recording of every work mentioned in the text. Even today a broad-cast commentator can draw on his station or personal record library for reproduced-sound illustrations of almost any composer and com-position he may discuss. But an author can only urge his readers to hear the music he writes about, saddling them with the burden of searching for pertinent, commercially available discs, or at least with the cost and effort of obtaining those he specifically recommends.

For a book like this, addressed primarily to non-specialist readers of perhaps comparatively little record-buying experience, definite listening suggestions are surely a necessity, yet I hesitate to provide them without some disclaimers and explanations. The former stem from my conviction, expressed earlier in these pages, that a record library is fundamentally a personal affair and outside recommenda-tions should be followed only insofar as they coincide with one's own musical tastes and needs. The explanations may be helpful in evaluat-ing my choices and, at least for some readers, in making the best practical use of the material presented in the following pages.

THE SELECTION OF RECORDED PERFORMANCES

Experienced or any other determinedly individualistic record col-lectors will have little if any need of my suggestions and indeed may have good grounds for preferring their own choices among the many available disc editions of most standard works. Comparative merits of different readings, performances, and recording techniques can be debated endlessly. However, these pages are hardly the place for that, especially since I expressly disclaim any attempt to compile a list of "best" or "definitive" versions, or for that matter to outline a "basic" library essential to every serious listener. My aim is merely to select specific LP recordings that represent, as satisfactorily as the repertory and my judgment permit, every composer and composition dealt with in this book.

Where my selections are not the only possible ones, they frankly represent an arbitrary choice among competing versions. In most cases this is my personal favorite; in some others (where I have no decisive preferences or have preferences I feel may be too individually prejudiced to be widely shared) I have followed the opinions of whatever other record critics I consider the most authoritative performance-judges of the particular music involved; in a few instances (where none of the available versions can be honestly recommended, or where I lack direct or indirect information on their merits) brackets are used to indicate a *faute de mieux* choice. But even this bracket warning should not be taken too seriously: by rigorous critical standards there probably are many other selections that should be bracketed, and for purely illustrative purposes most of the bracketed recordings probably are satisfactory enough.

Any reader who prefers to make his own choices is referred first of all to those literally indispensable tools for every LP-record buyer: the monthly catalogues (obtainable at most record shops) published by W. Schwann and the Long Player Publications. Discographically, neither is ideal and the latter in particular is downright slipshod at times, but both are invaluable practical handbooks except for the purpose of tracing small-scale works by the more obscure composers. For an incredibly detailed survey of the whole serious-music recorded repertory (at least up to 1951) one must turn to the monumental *World's Encyclopedia of Recorded Music* by Clough and Cuming, distributed in this country by the London Gramophone Company.

The phonographic literature includes a number of collections of critical evaluations, of which those by Hall, Kolodin, and Haggin probably are the best known, but unfortunately most of these were published before the LP repertory had begun to approach its present extent. However, several new "record books" are scheduled for publication in the fall or winter of 1953: Hall's and Levin's *The 1953 Guide to Good Listening* (Long Player Publications), Taubman's *How to Build a Record Library* (Garden City Press), and at least one other (Ballantine Books) on which I have not been able to obtain author and title information in time to include here.

Current record releases are reviewed, often in considerable detail, in many periodicals, among which even a brief list should include the *Saturday Review Recordings* (Kolodin and others), *American Record Guide* (Reed and others), *Gramophone Shop Supplement*, *High Fidelity* (Burke and others), *Library Journal* and *Consumer Reports* (Miller), *Musical Quarterly*, *Nation* (Haggin), *Audio Engineering* and *Harpers* (Canby), New York Sunday *Times* (Schonberg, Briggs, and others), New York Sunday *Herald Tribune* (Kupferberg and others), and — abroad — *The Gramophone* (London) and *Disques* (Paris). Reviews appearing in most of these and in some other publications are indexed, with symbols indicating the reviewers' opinions, by Kurtz Myers—quarterly in the Music Library Association journal, *Notes*, and every two years in paper-bound cumulations, obtainable through the Music Division of the Library of Congress, Washington 25, D. C.

Add the catalogues, bulletins, and advertisements of manufacturers and dealers, and it may be seen that today's record buyers need never be at a loss for phonographic information or critical opinion. To the inexperienced there well may seem to be an embarrassment of riches, but by trial and error it should not take anyone long to discover which sources are consistently most helpful for one's individual purposes.

And for the benefit of the complete novice only, a final note may not be entirely superfluous. The LP (that is, long-playing, 33⅓ rpm, microgroove) record has proved conclusively best suited for serious music. Old-style, 78-rpm, shellac records are rapidly becoming obsolete, and, though certain discs retain incomparable historical significance, many of these already have been or soon will be "transferred" to LP's. The 45-rpm microgroove discs, while suitable enough for small-scale serious works, generally only duplicate LP's in this repertory and need engage a record buyer's attention only if he is building a "popular" song and dance disc library. The following record lists are confined exclusively to long-playing editions. And though I have had to note for a few composers and works, "no LP's yet," it should be stressed that such statements invariably should be qualified by "to the best of my knowledge, as of July 1953." The repertory is expanding so fast these days that any present gap is likely to be filled in the near future, possibly even before these lines are published.

THE PRESENT INDEX-DISCOGRAPHY SCHEME

Quite apart from the choice of specific disc illustrations, a record list for this book posed special problems involving the following considerations: (1) the exceptionally large number of composers and works covered, however briefly, in the text; (2) the desirability of making the text itself as self-sufficient and as "readable" as possible; and (3) the exigencies of space, demanding the utmost economy of means to avoid allocating a disproportionate number of pages to record listing at the expense of those needed for text.

Reasons (1) and especially (2) ruled out the orthodox practice of supplying disc-edition references, either parenthetically or as footnotes, on the same page in which a composer or composition is first mentioned. And for reason (3) it was plainly impracticable (under given total-page limitations, already three-fourths expended on text) to achieve adequate completeness of detail in conventional back-of-the-book record lists and indexes.

It is perhaps too much to hope that the scheme of organization finally settled on will be immediately self-explanatory, but I trust that at least it will soon prove to be amply clear and convenient in practical use. The main thing to remember is that it *combines* the functions of index and discography, and that the latter function employs the minimum significant information essential to locating a particular disc in record catalogues or to ordering it, in person or by mail, from a record dealer.

The basic arrangement is an alphabetical sequence of proper names —primarily those of composers (printed in large and small capitals), but also including performers and authors specifically named in the text, plus a few of the less familiar instruments (such as lute, recorder, and viols). Each of these is accompanied by pertinent text-page references.

Musical works are not given main entries, but appear under their composers' names, in alphabetical sequence by title, form, or type, and these too are accompanied by text-page references. (General subjects are not indexed, as these may be traced easily enough either from the chapter headings listed on the contents page or via the composer or works with which they are most closely associated.)

Immediately following each musical work listed is a selected recorded performance, concisely identified by the name of the conductor, group, or principal performer, and the record-order number, both of which are printed in italics. The record manufacturer is indicated by a distinctive letter or group of letters, as specified in the code below, which also tabulates the comparatively few abbreviations used in the index-discography.

In addition, a few representative recordings are listed, when available, in the entries for the less familiar instruments mentioned above and the singers singled out for special mention on page 155 of the text. In the latter case, certain selections are bracketed less as non-recommendations than to indicate that these particular LP's unfortunately are uncharacteristic (in my opinion) of the artist's vocalism at its prime.

Record-Manufacturers' Code

AL	Allegro-Elite	C	Columbia
ARS	American Recording Society	CE	Classic Editions
		CH	Concert Hall Society
AS	Anthologie Sonore (in LP-preparation via the Haydn Society)	CI	Circle
		CR	Colosseum
		CS	Cetra-Soria
BG	Bach Guild	CT	Capitol (Telefunken)
BR	Bartók Records	D	Decca
BS	Bach Society	DI	Dial

E	Entre (via Columbia)	*PD*	Period
EMS	Elaine Music Shop	*PH*	Philharmonia
ES	Esoteric	*PO*	Polymusic
H	HMV (via RCA Victor)	*REB*	Robert E. Blake
HA	Handel Society	*RM*	Remington
HS	Haydn Society	*RN*	Renaissance
L	London	*S*	Stradivari
LY	Lyrichord	*SPA*	Society of Performing
M	Mercury		Artists
MGM	Metro-Goldwyn-Mayer	*U*	Urania
ML	Music Library	*V*	RCA Victor
NR	New Records	*VA*	Vanguard
OC	Oceanic	*VX*	Vox
OL	Oiseau-Lyre	*W*	Westminster

(*The names of other record manufacturers are spelled out.*)

Abreviations

abr.	abridged	in prep.	in preparation for early LP release
arr.	arranged (by or for)		
attr.	attributed to (i.e., a work of doubtful authenticity)	K.	Köchel index number
		mvt.	movement (of a larger work)
col.	collection (i.e., a group of pieces, usually three or more)	orch.	orchestra, or orchestrated (by)
		sel(s).	selection(s) (i.e., one or two examples)
harpsi.	harpsichord		
incid.	incidental music	#	number, No. (used for works in series)
incl.	including		

[ ] NOTE: recordings enclosed in brackets are *faute de mieux* choices: no other, or no better, recorded versions are available, yet I cannot honestly "recommend" these, either because they strike me as musically or technically inadequate for the particular music involved, or because I lack any information (direct or indirect) on their qualities.

Index-Discography

(BACH, J. S., continued)

—Cantatas, 4, 71, 134: #4, *Pro-haska, BG-511;* #56, *Ristenpart, D-9595;* #80, *Prohaska, BG-508;* #140, *Scherchen, W-5122;* #152, *Haas, W-5067;* #189, *Ludwig, D-9619.*

—Chorales, 134: sels., *Ross in C-2102.* (See also Cantata and Passion recordings.)

—Chorale-Preludes, 71, 134, 152: cols., *Viderø, HS-3063; Walcha, D-9569.*

—Clavierübung, 152: *Kirkpatrick & Callaway, HS-LA.*

—Concertos, 16, 71, 98, 141: harpsi., #1, *Istomin (piano), C-4309;* #4, #5 & #7, *Elsner, VX-7260;* 3 & 4 harpsi., *Heiller, HS-1024;* violin #2, *Busch, C-4002;* 2 violins, *Monteux, V-T1120;* violin & oboe, *Casals, C-4351.*

—English & French Suites, 71, 152: *Valenti, harpsi., W-A305 & W-A310.*

—Fugues, 26: Little G minor: *Stokowski (orch.) in V-1176;* col., *Münchinger (string orch.), L-526.*

—Geistliche Lieder, 158: sels., *Danco in L-698.*

—Goldberg Variations, 25, 152: *Kirkpatrick, HS-3062.*

—Inventions: *Kirkpatrick (clavichord), CH-1088.*

—Jesu, Joy of Man's Desiring, 12, 19: *Jacques in L-161.*

—Magnificat, 4, 41, 133: *Leitner, D-9557.*

—Mass, B minor, 4, 41, 71, 133: *Scherchen, W-A301.*

—Motets, 4, 136: *Thomas, CT-8077; Shaw, V-11; Ross, C-2102.*

—Musical Offering, 26, 41, 71: *Scherchen, W-5070;* Ricercare à 6 only, *Münchinger in L-526.*

—Oratorios, 4, 133: Christmas, *Grossmann, VX-7713;* Easter, *Prohaska, BG-507.*

—Organ works, 152: *Walcha, D series.*

—Partitas, 152: Kirkpatrick, *HS-3056/9.*—Passacaglia, 152: *Weinrich, MGM-3021.*

—Passions, 4, 41, 71, 133: St. John, *Grossmann, VX-6553;* St. Matthew, *Scherchen, W in prep.*

—Pastorale, 152: *White, M-15032.* — Preludes & Fugues (organ), 152: cols., *White, M-15027; Walcha, D-X117.*

—Sonatas, 150, 151: cello, *Casals, C-4349/50;* flute, *Baker, D-X113;* violin solo, *Schneider, M-GL1;* violin & harpsi., *Schneider, C-2109/11.*

—Suites, cello solo, 151: *Casals, V-T1104 & V in prep.*—Suites, orch., 8, 16, 71, 123, 141: #1, *Casals, C-4348;* #2 & #3, *Münchinger, L-313 & L-147;* #4, [*Koussevitzky, V-1079*].

—Toccatas & Fugues (organ), 32, 71, 152: C maj., *Schweitzer, C-4600;* D min., *Demessieux, L-319.*

—Transcriptions (orch.), 10-11: *Stokowski, V-1133, V-1176.*

—Trio-Sonatas (ensembles), 148: *Stern, C-4353; Rostal, CH-1174; Schneiderhan, W-5036;* (organ), 152: *Walcha, D-X114.*

—Well-Tempered Clavier, 71, 152: *Landowska, V series.*

BACH, W. F., 72, 76

—Concerto, piano, 139: *Thyrion, VX-6350.* — Sonata, harpsi., *Pinkham, AL-3037.*

—Trio-Sonatas, 148: *no LP's.*

Badura-Skoda, Paul, 17

BALAKIREV, 82 — Islamey (Casella): *Weldon, MGM-525.*—Thamar, 120: *no LP yet.*

CANNABICH, 77—Minuetto: *Stuttgart in RN-40*.

CANTELOUBE—Auvergne Songs, 156: *Grey, C-4459*.

CARISSIMI, 66
—Operas, 116: *no LP's yet.*
—Oratorios, 133: Jepthe, *Gerelli, VX-6100*; Jonas, *Gerelli, VX-7180*.
—Songs, 157: sel., *Cuénod in W-5059; Laszlo in W-5119*.

Carols, 136: cols., *Shaw, V-1112 & V-1711; Randolph, W-5100 & W-5200*. (See also Britten.)

CARPENTER, 90—Adventures in a Perambulator, 123; *Swoboda, CH-1140*.

Caruso, Enrico, 8, 9: cols., *V-T1007, V-T1034*, etc.

Catches & glees, 67, 158: cols., *Lewis, AL-3008, AL-3046*.

CESTI, 66—Opera air: *Laszlo in W-5119*.

CHABRIER, 83
—Duos, piano, 151: Valses, *Casadesus, C-2146*.
—España Rhapsody, 31, 122: *Ansermet in L-696*.
—Habanera, 30, & Ode, 36: *Fourestier in VX-7650*.
—Piano works, 153: col., *S. Stravinsky, AL-56*; sels., *Long in L-452*.
—Roi malgré lui, Danse slave, 119: *Jorda in L-191*.
—Songs, 160: sels., *Bernac in C-4484; Jansen in L-644*.
—Suite pastorale, 121: *Braithwaite, MGM-3000*.

Chaliapin, Feodor, 155: cols., *V-T3 (Boris Godunov), Audio Archives 77 /8*.

CHAMBONNIÈRES, 68—Harpsi. works: sels., *Chiasson in LY-19; Landowska in V-1217*.

CHARPENTIER, 89—Louise: *no large-scale LP yet.*

CHAUSSON, 86—Poème, 10, 121, 128: *Francescatti, C-2194*.—Songs, 160: sel., *Osborne, ML-7009*.—Symphony, 129: *Monteux, V-1181*.

CHÁVEZ, 93—Mexican col (incl. Paloma Azul), 25, 37: *Chávez, C-2080*.

CHERUBINI, 78—Requiem, 133: *[Davison, Program 705]*.—Symphony: *Toscanini, V-1745*.

CHOPIN, 80, 153-4.
—Ballades, 154: *Doyen, W-5169*.
—Berceuse, 35: *Novaes in VX-7810*.
—Concertos, piano, 97: #1, *[Brailowsky, V-1020]*; #2, *Novaës, VX-7100*.
—Etudes, 22, 154: Op. 10, *[Bailowsky in V-6000]*; Op. 25 *Novaës, VX-7560*.
—Fantaisie, 38, 154; *Novaës in VX-7810*.—Impromptus, 153: *Horszowski, VX-7870*.
—Mazurkas, 30, 123, 154: col., *Novaës, VX-7920*.
—Nocturnes, 35, 153: *Rubinstein, V-6005*.
—Piano works, 153-4: cols.: *Novaës, VX-7810; Cortot, H-1032; Moïséiwitsch, V-B1038; Pachmann et al., V-T1038*.
—Polonaises, 9, 153: *Rubinstein, V-1205, V-152*.
—Preludes: *Novaës, VX-6170*.
—Scherzos, 154: *Rubinstein, V-1132*.
—Sonatas, 151, 153: cello, *Kurtz, V-19*; piano #2 & #3, *Novaës, VX-7360*.
—Songs, 159: *Kurenko, LY-23*.
—Sylphides (arr. orch.), 120: *Desormière, L-192*.
—Waltzes, 30, 123, 153: *Lipatti, C-4522*.

CHRISTINÉ, HENRI—Phi-Phi,116: *Cariven, VX-20400*.

(Dvořák, continued)

—Serenades, 22, 140: Op. 22, *Von Benda, CT-8060;* Op. 44, *Haas, D-7533.*—Sextet, 146: *Jilka, RM-199-12.*

—Slavonic Dances, 30, 123: *Talich, U-604.*—Slav. Rhapsodies, 37: *Lehmann, D-4018.*

—Sonata, violin, 151: *Rybar, W-5015.*—Songs, 159: Biblical, *Duarte, ML-7024;* Duets, *Fuchs & Klose, U-5002.*

—Symphonies, 15, 25, 129: E flat, *Swoboda, W-5029;* #1, *Leinsdorf, C-4269;* #2, *Kubelik, H-1029;* #4, *Szell, L-488;* #5, *Szell, C-4541.*

—Trio, piano, 148: *Balsam, CH-1117.*

Dyson, Sir George, quoted, 113

ECCARD, 61—Motet: *Trapp in CH-1100.*

Eddy, Nelson, 9

Egyptian music (ancient), 53: *no LP's yet.*

Einstein, Alfred, 48 note

ELGAR, 86, 90

—Cockaigne Overture, 31: *Van Beinum, L-43.*—Concerto, violin, 128: *Heifetz, V-1090.*

—Enigma Variations: *Toscanini, V-1725.*—Oratorios, 132: *no LP's as yet.*

—Pomp and Circumstance Marches, 22: *Braithwaite in L-30.*

Eliot, T. S., quoted, 98, 148

ELLINGTON, 93; quoted, 107

—Sophisticated Lady, 12: *Ellington in C-4418.*

ENESCO, 90—Rhapsodies, 25: *Sevitzky, CT-8210.*

English Singers, 155: *no LP's.*

FALLA, 90

—Amor brujo, 31, 122: *Reiner,*

C-2006.—Concerto, harpsi., 140: *Kirkpatrick, M-10012.*

—Nights in the Gardens of Spain, 37: *Curzon, L-445.*

—Spanish Songs, 159: *Supervia, D-7510.*

—Three-Cornered Hat, 11, 31, 122: *Ansermet, L-598.*

—Vida Brève, Spanish Dance, 30: *Jorda in L-191.*

FARNABY, 64—Canzonets & Virginal works: *Hobbs & Winogron, EMS-5.*

FAURÉ, 83

—Pavane, 35: *no LP yet.*

—Piano works, 153: col., *Casadesus, C-2205.*

—Quartets, 145, 146: piano #1, *Casadesus, PO-1007;* string, Op, 121, *Guilet, PO-1008.*

—Quintet, piano, 145: *Lev, CH-1093.*—Requiem, 38, 133: *Leibowitz, OC-26.*

—Sonatas, 150: cello, *Soyer, PO-1007;* violin #1 & #2. *Fournier, W-5156.*

—Songs, 160: cols., *Danco, L-589, Vallin, VX-1730,* [*Panzéra, M-10097*]; sels., *Kolassi in L-568, Tourel in C-4158.*

—Trio, piano, 148: *Albeneri, M-10089.*

Ferrier, Kathleen, 19, 157: song cols.: *L-48, L-538.*

Fiedler, Arthur, 11, 18

FILTZ, 77: *no LP's yet.*

FINCK, 58, 61—Songs, 136: *Sacher, AS in prep.*

FLOTOW, 82—Martha; 116: *Rother, U-217.*

FOOTE, 86—Night Piece, 35, 145: *Baker, D-4013.*—Suite: *Hanson in M-40001.*

FOSTER, 83—Songs: *no recommended LP collections.*

FRANÇAIX, 92 — Concertino & Serenade, 140: *Françaix &*

Gilbert, W. S., 85 (See Sullivan for G & S operettas.)

GIORDANO, 86—Andrea Chénier, 116-17: *Paoletti, U-218.*

GLAZOUNOV, 89 — Concertos, 128, 140: saxophone, *Abato, PH-103;* violin, *Milstein, V-1064.*— Seasons, 120: *Desormière, CT-8157.*

GLIÈRE, 89-90—Red Poppy & Symphony "Ilya Murometz," 30, 122, 129: *Scherchen, W-A210.*

GLINKA, 82, 83—Life for the Tsar, 119: [*Melik-Pashayev, VA-6010/2*].—Sextet, 144: *Oborin, CR-104.*

GLUCK, 75-6
—Alceste: [*Leibowitz, OC-304*].
—Ballet Suite (arr. Mottl), 123: *Keilberth, U-7018.*
—Don Juan, ballet, 123: *Moralt, W-5028.*
—Orfeo, 115: in Italian, [*Rother, U-223*]; in French, abr., *Tomasi, VX-6780.*
—Overtures, 126: sels., *Kisch, L-9035.*

Goethe, 159; quoted, 13

GOLDMARK, 84—Rustic Wedding Sym., 129: *Beecham, C-4626.*

GOMBERT, 59—Motets, 136: sels., *Tinayre in D-X120.*

Goss, John (London Singers), 155: *no LP's.*

GOSSEC, 74—Quartet: *Loewenguth, AS in prep.*

GOTTSCHALK, 83—Cakewalk (Kay), 120: *Ormandy, C-4616.*
—Piano works: sel., *Behrend in AL-3024.*

GOUDIMEL, 60—Psalms, 136: sels., *Expert, AS in prep.*

GOULD, MORTON—Interplay, 123: *Gould, C-4218.*

GOUNOD, 82—Faust, 114, 119: *Beecham, V-T6100.*

GRAINGER, 90—Dances & folksong settings, 22-3, 123: *Stokowski, V-1238.*

GRANADOS, 86—Songs, 159: *Supervia, D-7510.* — Spanish Dances, 30, 123: *Echaniz, W-5181;* sels., *Jorda* (orch.) *in L-191.*

Greek (ancient) music, 52-3: sels., *Moser in D-X106.*

"Greensleeves," 9: see Vaughan Williams, fantasias.

Gregorian chant, 53-4, 56, 136-7: col., *Solesmes monks, L in prep.*

GRÉTRY, 74—Céphale et Procris, ballet suite (Mottl), 123: *André, CT-8135.*

GRIEG, 83
—Concerto, piano, 10, 97, 128: *Lipatti, C-4525.*—Dances, Norwegian & Symphonic, 23, 123: *Tuxen, M-10132.*
—Peer Gynt Suites, 15, 121: *Fiedler, V-7002.*
—Sonatas, 151: cello, *Rose, C-4652;* violin, #1 & #3, *Fuchs, D-9571.*
—Songs, 159: Haugtussa cycle, *Flagstad, V-1094;* col., *Flagstad, V-99.*

GRIFFES, 90—Piano works, 153: *Hambro, Walden 100.*—Poem, 35, 140: *Baker, D-4013.*

GROFÉ, FERDY—Grand Canyon, 35: *Toscanini, V-1004.*

HAHN, 86—Songs, 160: col., *Jansen, L-645.*

HALÉVY, 82—Juive, 117: sels., [*Slezak, Eterna 475*].

HALVORSEN—Boyards' March, 29: *Harrison in L-30.*

HAMMERSCHMIDT, 68—De Profundis, 134: *Warfield in C-4545.*
—Organ works, 152: *no LP's yet.*—Schaffe in mir (Motet): *Kugler in M-10087.*

(MENDELSSOHN, continued)

—Duos, clarinet & basset horn, 150: *Wlach, W-5024.*

—Midsummer Night's Dream, incid. music, 31, 35, 126: *Toscanini, V-1221.*

—Octet, 31, 146: *Stradivari, S-615;* scherzo only, arr. orch., *Busch, CH-61.*

—Oratorios, 81, 132: Elijah, *Sargent, C-SL155;* St. Paul, *no LP yet.*

—Overtures, 35: Fingal's Cave (Hebrides) & Ruy Blas, *Beecham, C-A7.*

—Quartets, string, 146: #3, *Stradivari, S-615.* — Quintets, string: #1 & #2, *Pascal, CH-1172.*

—Sonatas, 151: cello, *Graudan, VX-1710;* organ #6, *Schweitzer in C-SL175;* violin, *Guilet, CH-1095.*

—Songs, 159: cols., *Schumann, AL-51; Graf in CH-1159.*

—Symphonies, 11, 129: #3, *Steinberg, CT-8192;* #4, *Koussevitzky, V-20;* #5, *Prohaska, VA-425.*

—Trios, piano, 148: #1, *Rubinstein, V-1119.*

—Variations sérieuses, 25, 153: *Pelleg, CH-1127.*

MENOTTI, 93—Operas, 117: Consul, *Engel, D-X101;* Medium, *Balaban, C-SL154.*

MERBECKE, 62 — Anglican Communion: *Gilbert, C-4528.*

MERULO, 63 — Motet: *D'Alessio in VX-8030.*

MESSAGER, 86 — Veronique: *Gressier, VX-21100.*

MESSIAEN, 92 — Ascension: *Stokowski, C-4214.* — Organ works, 151: *White, M-10069, Watters, CE-1004.*

MEYERBEER, 82 — Huguenots, 117: *no recommended large-scale*

LP yet. — Patineurs Ballet (orch. Lambert), 120: *Irving, L-651.*

MIASKOVSKY, 90 — Symphonies, 129: #21, *Ormandy, C-4239.*

MILAN, 63 — Dances (arr.): *Miller in M-10003.*—Lute songs & solos, 158: *Cuénod & Leeb in W-5059.*

MILHAUD, 91, 92

—Boeuf sur le toit, 122: [*Mitropoulos, C-2032*]. — Concertino, violin, 140: *Kaufman, CT-8071.* —Création du monde, 36, 122: *Bernstein, C-2203.*

—Orestie, 132: *no LP yet.*

—Quartets, 145, 146: String, #1, *WQXR, PO-1004;* #14 & #15, *Budapest, C-4332;* wind & piano (sonata), *New York, EMS-6.*— Quintets, wind, 145: *New York, EMS-6.*

—Sacred Service, 132: *Weiner, CH-1103.* — Saudades, 37, 153: *Skolovsky, C-4523.*

—Symphonies, 129, 140: "Little," *Milhaud, CH-1076;* #1, *Milhaud, C-2082.*

—Trio (Suite), clarinet, 148: *Delecluze, PD-563.*

Milton, John, quoted, 131

Minnesänger, 55, 157 — Songs: sels., *Cape in ES-201, Rogers in AL-90, Moser in D-X106, Meili in AS in prep.*

Minstrels (medieval), 55—Songs: *Cape in EMS-201.*

MONSIGNY, 74: *no LP's yet.*

Monteux, Pierre, 11

MONTEVERDI, 66; 49, 61, 65

—Choral works, 133, 136: Beatus vir, *Ephrikian, PD-536;* Magnificat secundo, *Fleetwood, AL-3019;* Vespers, *Ephrikian, PD-558, Grischkat, VX-7902.*

—Madrigals, 158: Lagrime, *Couraud, VX-6670;* cols., *Boulanger,*

(MONTEVERDI, continued)
D-9627, Randolph, W-5171.

—Operas, 116: Combattimento,
Ephrikian, PD-551; Incoronazi-
one, Goehr, CH-1184; Orfeo,
[Koch, VX-6443].

—Songs, 157: sels., Boulanger in D-
9627, Laszlo in W-5119.

—Tirsi e Clori, 123: [Wenzinger,
CH-1085].

MORALES, 61—Motets, 136: sel.,
Holliday in NR-305.

Mörike, Eduard, 159

MORLEY, 62, 64

—Agnus Dei, 136: Shaw in V-136.

—Fantasias: sels., Recorder Consort in CE-1018.

—Madrigals, 62, 158: sels., Randolph in W-A212, CH-52.

—Songs: sels., Ferrier in L-807,
Cuénod in W-5085.

MOROSS, 93—Frankie and Johnny, 123: Hendl, ARS-12.

Mozarabic chant, 53: no LP's.

MOZART, 77-8, 2, 17, 18, 44, 60,
73, 74, 76, 84, 96, 116, 164

—Concertos, piano, 17-8, 78, 98,
128, 139: K.271, Hess, C-4568;
K.449, Istomin, C-4567; K.
450, no recommended LP; K.
466, Haskil, W-5054; K.467,
Demus, W-5183; K.482, Serkin,
C-4569; K.488, Gieseking, C-
4536; K.491 & K.595, Badura-
Skoda, W-5097; K.503, Fischer,
H-1004; K.537, Landowska,
V-T1029.

—Concertos, violin, 139: K.216,
Fournier, W-5187; K.218, Szigeti, C-4533; K.219, Morini, C-
4565.

—Concertos, wind insts., 17, 139:
bassoon, K.191, Sharrow, V-
1030; clarinet, K.622, Cahuzak,
HS-1047; flute, K.313, Wum-
mer, C-4567; horn, K.417 & K.
495, Brain, C-2088; K.447,

Jones, WCFM-8; oboe, K.314,
Saillet, RN-29.

—Dances (German & Contra)
123: cols., Litschauer, VA-426,
Leibowitz, ES-512.

—Divertimentos, 78, 139, 144,
147, 148: K.131, Blech, L-586;
K.251, Casals, C-4566; K.287,
Toscanini, V-13; K.334, Vienna,
L-235.—Divertimento, strings,
K.563; Pouget, W-5191. — Di-
vertimentos, winds only: K.
213, K.252-3, & K.270, Mayer-
hofer, W-5103; K.anh.229 (trios),
Wlach, W-5020, W-5022, W-5213.

—Duos, 151: piano, Badura-Skoda,
Wseries; strings, un-acc., K.423,
Goldberg, D-8523, K.424, Fuchs,
D-8510.

—Masses, 133: K.317, Messner,
Festival 100; K.427, Zallinger,
HS-2006; K.626 (Requiem),
Krips, L-230/1, or Scherchen, W
in prep.

—Motet, Exsultate, K.165, 133:
Troxell in WCFM-8.

—Operas, 38, 77, 115, 117, 119:
Cosí fan tutte, Busch, V-T6104;
Don Giovanni, Busch, V-T6102;
Entführung, Krips, L-A3; Ido-
meneo, Zellinger, HS-2020; Noz-
ze di Figaro, Busch, V-T6001;
Zauberflöte, Beecham, V-T6101.

—Overtures, 126: cols., Krips, L-
356; Bales, WCFM-3.

—Petites riens, ballet, 123: Reinhardt, VX-7250.

—Piano works, 152: cols. (incl.
Fantasia & Fugue, K.394, on
old pianos), Badura-Skoda, W-
5153, Kirkpatrick, BR-912. (See
also Sonatas, piano.)

—Quartets, piano, 145: K.478 &
K.493, Curzon, L-679.

—Quartets, string, 147: K.387,
Calvet, CT-8106; K.421, Hungarian, V-1076; K.458, Griller.

(MOZART, continued)
 L-658; K. 499 & K. 575, Stuy-
 vesant, PH-105.

—Quartets, with wind insts., 17,
 145: flute, K.285, etc., Baker,
 Oxford 101; oboe, K.370, Gom-
 berg, D-9618.

—Quintets, string, 42, 146: Budapest, C series.

—Quintets, with wind insts., 17,
 145: clarinet, K.581, Goodman,
 C-4483; horn, K.407, De Rosa,
 S-601; piano, K.452, no recommended LP.

—Serenades, 15, 78, 139, 144:
 K.239, Zimbler, D-8522; K.320,
 Maag, L-502; K.361 (13 winds),
 Vienna, VX-7470; K.375 & K.
 388, Vienna, VX-7490; K.525
 (Eine kleine Nachtmusik), Furt-
 wängler, H-1018.

—Sinfonie concertante, 121, 139:
 K.364 (strings), Casals, C-4564;
 K.anh.9 (winds), Reinhardt,
 VX-7320.

—Sonatas (Duos), 150: bassoon
 & cello, K.292, Oubradous, AS in
 prep.; violin, cols., Goldberg, D-
 X103, Barylli, W series; piano,
 Badura-Skoda, W series.

—Sonatas, organ & strings, 139:
 col., Messner, PD-534.

—Sonatas, piano, 152: K.310,
 Lipatti in C-4633; K.457 (with
 Fantasia, K.475), Firkusny, C-
 4356; K.533, Badura-Skoda in
 W-5153; K.570, Kirkpatrick in
 BR-912.

—Songs, 158: Danco, L-699.

—Symphonies, 42, 77, 78, 129,
 130, 139: early works, Acker-
 mann, CH series; K.183 & K.
 201, Wöldike, HS-1055; K.297,
 Beecham, C-4474; K.385, Van
 Beinum, L-214; K.504 & K.551,
 Beecham, C-4313; K.543 & K.
 550, Beecham, C-4674.

—Trios, 147 — clarinet, K.498,
 Kell, D-9543; piano, col., Jam-
 bor, PD-521/3. (For string trio,
 see Divertimento, K.563; for
 wind trios, see Divertimentos,
 K.anh.229.)

—Variations, piano, 152: K.354,
 Balsam in CH-1405; K.455,
 Foldes in VX-6810.

MUDARRA, 63—Harp Fantasia:
 Zabaleta in ES-509.—Lute songs
 & solo, 158: Cuénod & Leeb in
 W-5059.

Münchinger, Karl, 26

MUSSORGSKY, 82-3

—Boris Godunov, 38, 115: Do-
 browen, H-6400.

—Khovanshchina, 35, 119: Prelude, Entr'acte, & Persian
 Dances, Süsskind, MGM 3030.

—Night on Bald Mountain, 35:
 Ludwig in U-7035.

—Pictures at an Exhibition (orch.
 Ravel), 11, 127: Kubelik, M-
 50000.

—Songs, 160-1: col., Rosing, D-
 9577; Songs & Dances of
 Death only, Tourel, C-4289;
 Sunless and Nursery cycles, no
 LP's; col., Christoff, H-1033.

NANINO, 61 — Madrigals: col.,
 Fait, CR-1027. — Motets, 136:
 no LP's yet.

NARDINI, 75—Concerto, violin,
 139: Rybar, W-5049.

Negro Spirituals, 157: cols., Gold-
 en Gate Quartet, C-CL6102 &
 M-25063.

New Year's Concerts (Viennese),
 18: Krauss, L-484, L-683.

NICOLAI, 82—Lustige Weiber von
 Windsor, 117: Rother, U-214;
 Overture only, Beecham, C-A5.

NIELSEN, 90—Symphonies, 129:
 #1, Jensen, L-635; #6, Jensen,
 M-10137.

Nietzsche, Friedrich, quoted, 118
Noréna, Eidé, 155: *no LP's*.

OBRECHT, 58—Organ works: sel.,
Peeters in RN-39.—Sacred &
secular works, 136: *Cape, EMS-215-6 in prep.*

OCKEGHEM, 58, 59—Fugue, organ: *Peeters in RN-39.*—Sacred
& secular works, 136: *Cape,
EMS-210-1 in prep.*

OFFENBACH, 82
—Gaîté parisienne (Rosenthal),
11, 31: *Fiedler, V-1001.*—Helen
of Troy Suite (Dorati), 119:
Dorati, V-22.
—Operas, 114, 116: Contes
d'Hoffmann: *Beecham, L-A4.*—
Orphée aux envers: *Leibowitz,
RN-204.*

Onégin, Sigrid, 155: sel., in
V-T1115.

Organa, 54, 136: sels., *Cape in
EMS-201, AS in prep.; Tinayre
in D-X120.*

Orient, music of, 37, 53: col.,
[*Hornbostel, D-X107*].

PACHELBEL, 69—Organ works,
152: sel., *Supper in RN-202,
Nohren in AL-36.*

PADEREWSKI—Minuet in G, 8:
Paderewski in V-T10000.

PAGANINI, 81
—Caprices, violin solo, 151: *Ricci,
L-252, L-264.*
—Concertos, violin, 128: #1,
Francescatti, C-4315; #2, *Menuhin, H-1015.*
—Quartet, string, 146: *Guilet, CH
in prep.*

PAISIELLO, 75—Opera airs: sels.,
Barbieri in VX-7980.

PALESTRINA, 60; 49, 61, 65, 131
—Madrigals, 158: sels., *Opienski,
AS in prep.*—Magnificat, 136:
Russell in Festival 70-202.

—Masses, 136: "Marcellus,"
[*Wagner, CT-8126*]; cols., [*Welch,
AL-70, AL-3016*].
—Motets, 136: cols., *Bartolucci,
RN-55*; sels., *Welch in LY-35,
Woodworth in Cambridge 101.*

Panzéra, Charles, 155: cols.,
[*M-10097, M-10098*].

PARADISI, 75—Sonata mvt.: *Joyce
(piano) in D-7513.*

PASQUINI, 67—Aria: *De Luca in
D-7505.*—Harpsi. works, 152:
no LP's yet.

PEPUSCH, 74: Beggar's Opera,
116: *Goberman, Desto 1.*

PERGOLESI, 75
—Concertos, 140, 141: flute,
Meylan, CH-1082; orch., #4,
Münchinger, L-312, #5, *Fasano
in D-9598*, "Trio-Sonata," *Moralt in W-5009.*
—Operas, 75, 116: Music Master
(in English), *Woodhouse, L-291*;
Serva Padrona, *Simonetto, CS-50036.*
—Song (attr.): *Laszlo in W-5119.*
—Stabat Mater, 133: [*Grischkat, PD-530*].

PERI, 65—Opera airs: sel., [*Souzay in L-731*], [*De Luca in Continental 102*].

PEROTINUS, 54—Sacred works,
136: col., *Boepple, CH-1112*; sels.,
*Cape in EMS-201, Warfield in
C-4545.*

PEZEL, 69—Sonatas, etc., for
brass: cols., *Schuller, EMS-7,
Schuman, PD-526.*

PFITZNER, 85—Overtures: *Rother
& Pfitzner, U-7050.*—Symphonies: *Böhm & Abendroth, U-7044.*

PICCINI, 75: *no LP's yet.*

PIERNÉ, 86—March of the Little
Lead Soldiers, 29: *Hendl in
C-4118.*—Sonata, violin: *Fiqueroa, NR-401.*

*Works starred also exist in piano
versions and are included in
the Casadesus series of Ravel's
complete piano works.

(RAVEL, continued)
CH-1123.—Sonatine: see piano works.

—Songs, 36, 156, 160: Chansons madécasses, *Jansen in L-644;* Don Quichotte, *Singher in C-4152;* Histoires naturelles, *Bernac in C-4333;* Shéhérazade cycle, *Tourel, C-4289.*

—Tombeau de Couperin*, 121: *Reiner in V-1724.*—Trio, 148: *Rubinstein, V-1119.*

—Valse, 25, 121: *Ansermet, L-22.* —Valses nobles*, 121: *André, CT-8132.*

—(See also Mussorgsky, Pictures at an Exhibition.)

Reading Rota (Sumer is i-cumen in), 56: *no LP yet.*

Recorders, 62, 63, 150: cols., *Consort,CE-1018; Dolmetsch,L-24, L-278.* (See Bach, Handel, et al.)

REGER, 85—Variations and Fugue (Mozart), 25, 26: *Van Beinum, D-9565.*

REINCKEN, 68—Harpsichord work: *Weiss-Mann in AL-52.*

RESPIGHI, 90

—Ancient airs & dances, 123: Suite #2, *Litschauer, VA-433;* #3, *Münchinger, L-312.*

—Fountains & Pines of Rome, 37: *Quadri, W-5167.*

REZNIČEK, 85—Donna Diana, Overture only: *Fistoulari in MGM-120.*

RICHARD THE LION-HEARTED, 55 —Song: *Meili, AS in prep.*

RICHTER, 77—Quartet, string: *New Music, BR-915.*

RIMSKY-KORSAKOV, 82

—Antar, 36: *Leinsdorf, C-2044.*

---

*Works starred also exist in piano versions and are included in the Casadesus series of Ravel's complete piano works.

—Capriccio espagnol & Coq d'or Suite, 30, 36, 37, 121: *Desormière, CT-8155.*

—Concertos, 97, 128: piano, *Badura-Skoda, W-5068;* trombone, *Shuman, CI-51-103.*

—Quintet, piano, 145: *Raupenstrauch, W-5019.*

—Russian Easter Overture, 37: *Cluytens in VX-7670.*

—Scheherazade, 36, 120: *Monteux, V-1002.*—Snow Maiden, ballet, 30, 119: *Ludwig, U-7035.*

—Tati-Tati (with Borodin, et al.), 25: *Janssen, C-4480.*

RODGERS, 93—Oklahoma, 116: *Blackton, D-8000.*

ROMBERG, 90—Student Prince: col., *Engel, C-4592.*

Rome (ancient), music of, 53: *no LP's.*

ROSENMÜLLER, 69—Suite, 141: *Sachs, AS in prep.*—Trio-Sonata: *Harpsi. Qt., ES-517.*

ROSSINI, 81

—Boutique fantasque (Respighi), 120: *Ansermet, L-274.*—Matinées & Soirées musicales (Britten), 120: *Braithwaite, MGM-3028.*

—Operas, 31, 114, 116, 119: Barbiere di Siviglia, *Previtali, CS-1211;* Cenerentola, [*Rossi, CS-1208*]; Guglielmo Tell, *Rossi, CS-1232;* ballet only, *Serafin in V-B1039.*

—Oratorio, Mosè in Egitto, 132: *no LP yet.*

—Overtures, 31, 126: cols., *Toscanini, V-1044; Van Beinum, L-358.*

—Quartets, wind, 145: *New Art, CE-1010.*

—Stabat Mater, 133: *Sternberg, OC-24.*

ROUSSEAU, 74; quoted, 79

—Opera airs: *Angelici, AS in prep.*

Schoenberg, 88, 90
—Erwartung, 156: *Dow, C-4524.*
—Kammersymphonie, 140: *Dervaux, DI-2.*—Organ Variations, 151: *Watters, CE-1004.*
—Piano works, 153: cols., *Field, PD-568, Steuermann, DI-14.*—Pierrot Lunaire, *Schoenberg, C-4471.*
—Quartets, string, 146: *Juilliard, C in prep.*—Quintet, wind: *Met., DI-13.*
—Serenade, 140: *Mitropoulos, ES-501.*—Trio, string, 148, *Koldofsky, DI-3.*
—Verklärte Nacht, 121, 146: sextet, *Hollywood, CT-8118;* orch., *Ormandy, C-4316.*

Scholes, Percy, 47

Schubert, 78-9, 84
—Dances, 123: German, cols., *Leibowitz in ES-512, Moralt, VX-7280, Stokowski in V-1238;* Ländler, *Kraus, D-8505.*
—Duos, piano, 151: cols., *Badura-Skoda, W-5047, W-5093, W-5147; Vronsky, C-2125.*
—Impromptus, Opp. 90 & 142, 153: *Schnabel, H-1027.*
—Marche militaire, 29: *no recommended LP.*—Masses, 133: #6, *Moralt, VX-7840.* — Moments musicaux, 153: *Demus, RM-149-21.*
—Octet, 144: *Vianna, W-5094.*
—Part-songs, 158: cols., *Shaw, V-81, Grossmann, VX-6870.*
—Quartets, string, 147: *Vienna Konzerthaus, W series.*—Quintets, 25, 145, 146: piano ("Forellen"), *Horszowski, C-4317;* string (Op. 163), *Budapest, C-4437.*
—Rosamunde, incid. music, 123: *Dixon, W-5182;* overture (Zauberharfe), 15: *Van Beinum in L-622.*

—Sonatas, 150, 153: cello (Arpeggione), *Feuermann, C-4677;* piano, *Aitken, EMS series in progress;* violin, #1, *Szigeti, C-4133,* #5, *Menuhin, V-140.*
—Songs, 8, 9, 157, 158-9: Schöne Müllerin, *Schiøtz, V-T1048;* Schwanengesang (excerpts), *Fischer-Dieskau in H-1046;* Winterreise, *Carne, W-5087 /8;* col. (incl. Ave Maria & Ständchen), *Anderson, V-98;* col., *Schlusnus, L-106.*
—Symphonies, 16, 19, 32, 79, 129, 130, 140: #2, *Steinberg, CT-8161;* #4, *Van Beinum, L-736;* #5, *Busch, CH-61;* #6, *Krips, L-21;* #8 ("Unfinished") *Krips, L-209;* #9 (or "7," C major), *Furtwängler, D-X119.*
—Trios, piano, Opp. 99 & 100, 16, 147: *Badura-Skoda, W-5188, W-5121.*

Schütz, 68
—Cantatas & sacred airs, 134: col., *Cuénod, W-5043;* sel., *Warfield in C-4545.*
—Motets, 136: col., *Grossmann in VX-6860;* sel., *Shaw in V-1201.*
—Passions, "Stories," etc., 134: Christmas, *Mendel. REB-3;* Requiem, *Mendel. REB-9;* Resurrection. *Schleiffer, M-10073;* St. Matthew, *Koch, BG-519 /20;* Seven Words, *Grossmann, VX-6860.*

Schultz, 78: *no LP's yet.*

Schuman, William
—Ballets, Judith & Undertow, 123: *Whitney & Schuman, M-10088.* — Quartets, 146: #3, *Juilliard, C-4493.*
—Symphonies, 130: #3, *Ormandy, C-4413;* strings, *Steinberg, CT-8212.*

Schumann, Elisabeth, 155: see Franz & Mendelssohn songs.

. . . So when we have travell'd as farre as wee can, with safetie, that is, as farre *as* Ancient, *or* Modern Expositors *lead us, in the* discoverie *of these* new Heavens, *and* new Earth, *yet wee must say at last, that it is a* Countrey *inhabitated with* Angells, *and* Arch-angells, *with* Cherubins, *and* Serephins, *and that wee can looke no farther into it, with these eyes.*
—DONNE: *A Sermon (July 1, 1627)*

Acknowledgments

THE FREQUENCY with which the word *I* dots these pages and the prevailing stress on personal views cannot—and are not intended to—conceal my obvious obligation to the researches, ideas, and judgments of many other writers. It would be impossible for me to specify even those debts I am consciously aware of, and in many instances the sources themselves might rightfully disclaim all responsibility for the metamorphoses their original materials have undergone as reworked in my mind and words. Somewhat similarly, while most of the notions explicitly or implicitly advanced here probably stem from earlier formulations somewhere in my own books, articles, and reviews, their evolution has been so tortuous that it would be of doubtful service to credit the first appearances, even if I could locate them all.

Fortunately, more direct acknowledgments can be paid to the authors and publishers of the heterogeneous books from which I have drawn the brief quotations that serve as epigraphs—if not as text springboards—for my chapters here. Also to the record manufacturers who have been generous sources of both information and discs; to the authors, compilers, and publishers of currently available record reviews, books, and catalogues enumerated in the preliminary notes to my index-discography; and especially to Philip L. Miller and Harold C. Schonberg, whose phono-musical knowledge and personal friendship no demand of mine has been able to exhaust.

Innumerable other friends have contributed, knowingly or unknowingly, to my estimates of listeners' most pressing interests and problems, but of these I must limit myself to singling out Charlotte and Richard Gilbert, Lewis M. Patlin, Mary and John Marshall, Hans H. Fantel Emily and Graydon Walker, Hal Webman, Elaine Keehn, and my sister, Josephine Darrell Holmes.

And, finally, I owe more than conventional thanks to my present editor, Herbert Weinstock, and others among my publisher's staff, for their skill in coping not only with the normal problems of book production, but also with the sometimes quite novel ones in which I have involved them here. —R. D. D.

A NOTE ON THE TYPE

This book is set in Monotype BASKERVILLE, *a facsimile cutting from type cast from the original matrices of a face designed by John Baskerville. The original face was the forerunner of the "modern" group of type faces.*

John Baskerville (1706–75), of Birmingham, England, a writing-master, with a special renown for cutting inscriptions in stone, began experimenting about 1750 with punch-cutting and making typographical material. It was not until 1757 that he published his first work, a Virgil in royal quarto, with great-primer letters. This was followed by his famous editions of Milton, the Bible, the Book of Common Prayer, and several Latin classic authors. His types, at first criticized as unnecessarily slender, delicate, and feminine, in time were recognized as both distinct and elegant, and his types as well as his printing were greatly admired. Four years after his death Baskerville's widow sold all his punches and matrices to the Société Littéraire-typographique, which used some of the types for the sumptuous Kehl edition of Voltaire's works in seventy volumes.

Composed by W. F. Hall Printing Co., Chicago, Ill. Printed and bound by H. Wolff, New York.